Daniel Harbour read mathematics and
philosophy at Balliol College, Oxford,
and is currently writing his doctoral
thesis in Linguistics at MIT.

D1104490

An Intelligent Person's
Guide to Atheism

An Intelligent Person's Guide to Atheism

DANIEL HARBOUR

Duckworth

First published in 2001 by
Gerald Duckworth & Co. Ltd.
61 Frith Street, London W1D 3JL
Tel: 020 7434 4242
Fax: 020 7434 4420
Email: enquiries@duckworth-publishers.co.uk
www.ducknet.co.uk

A catalogue record for this book is available
from the British Library.

ISBN 0 7156 2915 8

Typeset by Derek Doyle & Associates, Liverpool
Printed in Great Britain by
Biddles Ltd, *www.biddles.co.uk*

Contents

Acknowledgements

In researching and writing this book and in thinking and talking about the issues it addresses, I have become indebted to many people in many ways. In sitting down to record my debt, I have the pleasure of remembering much time spent in discussion with family, friends, and colleagues. Without their contributions I doubt this book would have been written.

The first to be thanked must be my family. My parents have always encouraged me to look for questions, to question answers, and to have confidence enough to offer my own. My interest in the topic of this book stems in part from their opposing views on the matter, views that they were always happy to explain to me without any attempt to make me adopt them. In similar ways, I am also grateful to my brothers and my other family: grandparents, aunts, uncles, cousins, and others for whom there is, unfortunately, no exact term. Most significant of these is Dirk Hannemann, who, like everyone else in this paragraph, it is beyond me adequately to thank.

Many friends have had substantial influence on this book. Most concretely, Melvin Claridge's persistent questions, by turns profound and frivolous, first needled me into formulating the precise arguments presented here. I remember his musing at one point, 'Sounds like you need to write a book'; my response was that if he did not watch out, I would. As it is, he didn't so I did. Christians have been very important to my understanding of atheism, theism and related issues, specifically, Chris Hooley and Christian List. My friendship with both began with my university studies and has been a source of joy and stimulation. In reading the current version of the manuscript, I find much that can be traced directly back to talks and walks with them in parks in Oxford and Boston or at dinners and late nights in the same places. Similarly, I have to thank Andrew Clark and John Dyke, Noam Bar and Yotam Ottolenghi.

Also from Oxford, I must thank three philosophers who have been strong influences: Jim Higginbotham, Bill Newton-Smith, and Alex Rosenberg. Much of what I regard as constituting good questions come from observing them. I am sure that, without them and my many other tutors at Oxford and teachers at school, I would not be where I am now.

At the Massachusetts Institute of Technology, I have found myself part of an extremely exciting and welcoming environment. My colleagues' enthusiasm for this project – which, to be frank, has little to do with what I am meant to be doing at MIT – has seen me through several fraught moments. For comments on earlier drafts, I am grateful to David Adger and Jay Rifkin, and for their general interest and encouragement, to Noam Chomsky, María Cristina Cuervo, Adam Elga, Little Doe Fermino, Ken Hale, Elizabeth Harman, Sabine Iatridou, Tatjana Marvin, and Anthony Newman. Of the aforementioned, I must single out Noam Chomsky, to whom I recognise a particular debt. His writings on the history and philosophy of science, particularly in relation to linguistics, have been crucial to the formulation of my views about what constitute the real issues in the (a)theism debate and where their answers are likely to lie. It is fair to say that this book would have nothing like its current form or content without him.

My aim to mount an argument for atheism, as opposed to an argument against theism, has been greatly aided by Robin Baird-Smith. His insightful comments led me to consider more carefully the practical implications of my arguments. I wonder whether I would have thought to write anything like Chapter 6 without his input. For access to parliamentary records and speeches, I am grateful to Arun Kataria, in the Press Office of Lambeth Palace, and Simon Blundell, librarian of the Reform Club.

I dedicate this book with love and thanks to my grandparents, Sidney and Fay Harbour, and Emanuel and Elizabeth Kaye, and with love and hope to my godchildren, Bracha and Jacob Eisenstat. I hope through this book to contribute to the latter's compassion and understanding as the former have contributed to mine.

Introduction

Atheism is the plausible and probably correct belief that God does not exist. Opposed to atheism, there is theism, the implausible and probably incorrect view that God does exist. This book is about why atheism is correct, why theism is incorrect, and why anyone who cares about truth should be an atheist.

Almost everyone has had discussions about whether God exists. They usually follow the same well-beaten path. A theist points to a wonderful, remarkable occurrence, such as a beautiful coincidence, and claims that it provides evidence of God. An atheist responds that coincidences provide no solid evidence, then points to an appalling, remarkable occurrence, such as a disaster, and claims that it provides evidence against God. The theist retorts that disasters and God are hardly incompatible, appealing perhaps to a divine plan or to divine inscrutability. And so the gainsaying goes, back and forth. However, after several such discussions, most people reach the same conclusion: one cannot prove that there is a God, and one cannot prove there is not. As this is a point beyond which argumentation cannot progress, the question of belief is left to the individual's discretion, or indiscretion, as the case may be, and atheists and theists settle for an accommodating compromise, each thinking the other wrong, but unassailably so.

Particularly among scholars, accommodation has become the norm. The following passage by John Searle neatly sums up the sentiment.

> John Stuart Mill and Bertrand Russell mounted polemical and eloquent attacks on traditional religion. Nowadays nobody bothers, and it is considered in slightly bad taste even to raise the

question of God's existence. Matters of religion are not to be discussed in public.[1]

As the passage indicates, it is regarded today as improper to hold God up to too close a scrutiny. It is a shame that an issue of such fundamental importance and interest should have become an embarrassment, an issue not to be aired in public. That it has is doubtless in part recognition of the staleness of discussions in the mould described above and the deadlock to which they lead. Frustrated by the futility, I too left the fray and became an accommodating atheist.

In this book, I return to the fray for a simple reason. I have realised that accommodating atheism, though popular, is wrong. Specifically, it involves two errors, one factual and one moral. The factual error is the claim that atheism and theism are both equally plausible given all the evidence, that they are of the same logical pedigree. In fact, they only seem to be equal if you base the debate on the wrong question. Traditional discussions portray the difference between atheism and theism as consisting in nothing more than answering 'Does God exist?' differently. Of course, they do answer that question differently. However, our commitment to atheism or to theism arises from something much more fundamental, namely the whole worldview to which we subscribe. First, we must consider what constitutes a coherent and sensible way to look at the world and our place within it. Only then can we sensibly ask what God's place is in our worldview. If we ask these more fundamental questions, it will become clear, I argue, that atheism makes sense in a way in which theism fails to. That is, it will become clear that simply and logically atheism is superior to theism.

There are probably as many beliefs about God as there are people to hold them. So, the claim that atheism is superior to theism is too vague to mean much. It is important to clarify exactly what it is that I will argue for and what it is that I will argue against. I shall argue for an atheism rooted in the paradigm of rational enquiry, the paradigm in which we conduct our philosophy, mathematics and natural science, and, ever increasingly, our social and cognitive science, our ethics and aesthetics. This is essentially a philosophy of the Enlightenment. And I shall attack theism construed broadly so as to include not only religions of long standing and their younger offshoots, but also the fashionably vague notion of some 'power' or 'energy' or 'force' at the heart of today's modern, brand-less spiritualism.

This book is about two different worldviews and the role that atheism and theism play within them. In it, I will argue for atheism indirectly. To begin with, I consider what worldviews are, and why we need them. This may sound terribly abstract and philosophical, but it is not. The discussion will be kept concrete by considering two particular worldviews, that are equal and opposite. I show two facts about these worldviews. Firstly, that one of them is sensible and plausible, and that the atheism described above is an instance of it. From this, it follows that atheism is plausible and probably correct. Secondly, that the other worldview is neither sensible nor plausible, and that theism broadly construed is an instance of it. From this, it follows that theism is implausible and probably incorrect. The opening chapters of the book, where this argument is presented, therefore constitute an initial proof of atheism's superiority over theism.

People rightly require more from a worldview than logical pedigree and plausibility, however. Such philosophical frameworks must be conducive to a good life, to happiness and morality. Therefore, in the middle chapters of the book, I consider which of the two opposing worldviews fares better on this score. That is, as the book progresses, we turn away from questions of pure philosophical soundness to issues of practical efficacy. By considering a wide range of evidence, historical and ethical, aesthetic and personal, I show that the logical superiority of atheism over theism, or of one worldview over its opposite, is replicated at the practical level. So, this provides a second argument for the preferableness of atheism.

I said that I had ceased to be an accommodating atheist for two reasons, one factual and one moral. The factual one should now be clear: both at the theoretical level and at the practical, atheism is superior to theism. So, there is no impasse in argumentation, no philosophical plateau, and so no need for a tactical compromise. In the final chapters, I turn to the moral error of accommodation.

Newspapers, radio and television often publicise clerics' opinions on current affairs. Religious doctrine and sentiment are in the mouths of politicians and in the minds of think-tanks. If there, they are also surely on the statute book. So, while the atheist is not debating the worth of religion, while he or she is being accommodating, the theist is busy influencing politics and society on the basis of his or her beliefs. The atheist's unilateral withdrawal from the argument leaves the opportunity and power to shape society in the hands of the opponent. Yet, if there are good and sound reasons to be atheist, then there are good and sound reasons not to be a theist, and so there are good and sound reasons not to allow theism in the shape of religion and the religious to influence the shape of society. Conversely, there are like reasons to increase the influence of atheist thought. This is underlined by the second of the above arguments for atheism: it and the worldview to which it belongs are more conducive to morality than theism, so, if one is to have greater influence in society, it is atheism. This argument is developed by examining the role that religion has played in three movements fundamental to our modern conception of morality and to our social and democratic ideals: the abolition of slavery, the emancipation of Jewry, and the enfranchisement of women. In all these cases, history carries the warning that religion and religious sentiment are often impediments and rarely really allies to moral progress.

Throughout the book, the fuel for my arguments, as already evident, comes from a wide variety of sources: philosophy and psychology, mathematics and science, history and art, religion and theology. In touching on so many areas, and in undertaking so large a project in so small a space (this book is intended to be read in a comfortable afternoon beside a swimming pool), there must be many issues and subtleties that are ignored. In making the argument streamlined and surveyable, a certain fine-grainedness is sacrificed. However, this is not simplification to the point of error. I am confident that the reader will find the most significant issues concerning this 'new' (a)theism debate adequately identified and dealt with below and that what is not discussed can be fitted into the rubric of the argument I present.

One final word. I have often felt that many atheists fall into to the trap of simply attacking theism. You may recall Searle's mention of Mill and Russell's 'polemical and eloquent attacks'. I intend this book to present a positive argument for atheism, rather than merely a negative argument against its opposite. By tying the debate between atheism and theism to more fundamental questions about worldviews, I hope to show that we ought to be atheists in virtue of our basic desire to understand ourselves and the world of which we are part.

Chapter 1

Basics and Basis

In the beginning ... – Genesis 1:1

Atheism, Theism, and Superiority

Traditionally, the debate between atheism and theism is a matter of attempted proof and disproof. Attempts to prove God's existence include the Argument from First Cause and the Argument from Design. Attempts to disprove God's existence include the Argument from Suffering. However, such debates miss the point and the result is a boring and futile discussion. In this book, I shall not try to prove atheism true nor theism false. Rather, I want to show that atheism is 'superior' to theism.

'Superior' may seem an odd word to use in this context. It is clear what is meant by saying that one view is true and another false, or one view correct and another incorrect. I use the word 'superior' deliberately though. Proofs of truth and falsity are rare things. One can only prove something relative to a set of assumptions or facts. One assumes such-and-such and proves so-and-so on that basis. However, what is at stake in the (a)theism debate is not whether God's existence follows from the fact that the world is beautiful and intricate, nor whether God's non-existence follows from the fact that people suffer. Nor is the debate about whether there is a set of facts that would clinch the matter for either side.

Rather, the debate needs to be reoriented to a much more fundamental issue: the whole worldview to which we subscribe. Worldviews, our basic assumptions about ourselves and our world, respond to a fundamental human need: the desire to understand. I will present two opposite worldviews, called the

Spartan meritocracy and the Baroque monarchy, for reasons that will soon be apparent, arguing that one is clearly superior to the other, in the sense that only one presents a plausible way to gain understanding. Atheism's superiority to theism will then follow because of atheism's relationship to the superior Spartan meritocracy and theism's relationship to the inferior Baroque monarchy.

In the next section, I will show firstly why worldviews are so important and will then introduce the two worldviews that will be central to this book. Although the terms 'Spartan meritocracy' and 'Baroque monarchy' may sound unfamiliar and the appeal to worldviews, overly abstract, manifestations of both surround us and can be shown to be quite familiar. The remaining sections and the next chapter focus on the worldviews' relationship to atheism and theism, showing how the superiority of one worldview over the other is, in fact, the superiority of atheism over theism.

Two Worldviews

Humans love to explain things. True universals of human nature are rare, yet our passion for explanations is surely one of them. Seemingly every society and culture has stories to explain where we and the world come from, to explain regular occurrences, such as sunrise and sunset, the passage of seasons, the mechanisms of birth and death, and to explain more haphazard events, such as sudden fortunes or flash floods.

This urge to explain reveals two fundamental facts about us. One is that we are ignorant, and the second is that we dislike our ignorance. So, if we are going to seek a cure for our ignorance, what is the best way to do it?

Fortunately, the answer is very simple: we cure ignorance by discovering truth. Unfortunately, discovering truth is no simple business. However, a large number of people have gone before us and done much of the hard work. We are taught a large number of facts, home truths and hard truths, that have accumulated over the generations. But if we had to start from the beginning, building a new explanation of everything, how would we satisfy the human urge to explain?

We meet our urge to explain by adopting a worldview. Worldviews are not explanations in themselves; they are not theories. They are the foundations on which explanations are built. To see what this means, suppose that you have realised, after long, hard work, that there are no such things as atoms. You prove the claim, say, by observing that if there are atoms, then the world should behave one way whereas in reality it behaves another. In other words, you conduct some form of experiment. But the proof only works if you make certain assumptions about the experiment and what its results mean. You can try to justify your interpretation of the experiment by using yet another proof. But then the same questions arise about whether the interpretation is correct and whether the new assumptions are justified. There is some merit in digging deeper, in scrutinising as finely as possible. Yet, at some point, there must come an end. One cannot go on justifying one's assumptions forever, because, even if there are enough reasons, there is not enough time. Somewhere one has to assume something. This is what I mean by a worldview, a set of assumptions about the nature of the world, on the basis of which one can begin to attempt to understand other aspects of the world.

So, one has to make some assumptions. The question is which. For a first attempt, we would make a stab, a step in the dark and see how things developed. There is, after all, no alternative. We can, however, form views right at the outset about two important issues: how many starting assumptions we should make, and how we should regard our starting as our explanations encounter contrary realities. The first issue concerns the judiciousness of taking a very elaborate starting assumptions position when we are still largely ignorant about the world; whether we should be Spartan or Baroque. The second issue concerns our reaction to discoveries that contradict our initial explanation of the ways and whys of the world. For instance, on the one hand, we may decide that our initial assumptions are not to be revised under any circumstances and that all embellishments and extensions of the explanation must not undermine our starting position. That is, we may treat our starting assumptions as monarchs to which everything else is secondary. On the other hand, we may regard everything, whether starting assumption or later addition, as equal and equally subject to reexamination, reevaluation and rejection. That is, we may be strictly meritocratic, regarding every part of our growing explanation as provisional and in need of constant testing for worthiness and worth.

It is here that the difference between atheism and theism will become apparent. As already outlined, there are two types of worldview one could take: the Spartan and the Baroque. To elaborate slightly, a good Spartan worldview would make the minimal number of assumptions. It would not say what there is, nor would it say what there is not. All it provides is a set of methods for finding out about how the world behaves and what there is in it. On the other hand, a Baroque worldview would be richly embellished, coming complete with a set of beliefs about what exists, why those things exist, how they came to exist, and so on. The potential differences between worldviews continues when it comes to their application, that is, when we build explanations of the world using them as a basis. In a meritocratic worldview, every assumption about the world must work and must be seen to work. If a method of explaining the world leads to contradictions, then it is discarded. If the assumption that the world contains such-and-such is useless, then it is discarded. Everything must merit its place in one's picture of the world. This includes the basic assumptions in the worldview too: not even they are immune from criticism, revision, or rejection. In a monarchic worldview, by contrast, a certain set of assumptions is privileged in that one must accept them as true. If one's experience or commonsense or intuition or logic contradicts the creed, then the fault lies, not with the privileged beliefs, but with experience, commonsense, intuition, and logic. In constructing one's explanation of the world, the nature of explanation must always remain subservient to the assumptions of the worldview.

The kernel is that there are two ways to look at the world. One starts with minimal assumptions and recognises that they may be wrong and need revision. The other starts with a rich view of the way the world is and forbids revision of the basic assumptions. The two most opposite worldviews we can adopt are, therefore, the Spartan meritocracy and the Baroque monarchy. In the Spartan monarchy, the starting position is as modest as possible and all is provisional and must prove its worth. In the Baroque monarchy, the starting assumptions are intricate, complex and immune from revision in the light of later data. (Of course, there are two other positions, the Baroque meritocracy and the Spartan monarchy. Although there are obvious conflicts between the status of the starting assumptions and later assumptions in the positions, they are interesting enough to deserve some discussion. See, in particular, the passages on Michurinism and Islamic Science.)

Recall what the purpose of adopting a worldview is: to provide the basis on which to build an explanation and an understanding of the world. It should be clear which of the Spartan meritocracy and the Baroque monarchy is better placed to meet our urge to explain. The desire to explain things is an admission of ignorance. So, the starting position is infected with ignorance. It is inevitably wrong. So, we should be prepared to recognise it as such and to revise it when it is possible to increase its accuracy. In order to minimise the scope for error, and in order to locate the source of such errors when they emerge, initial assumptions are best kept to a surveyable minimum. Alternatively, it is either arrogance or folly to assume that an uninformed guess at the nature of Nature will be or should be beyond need of revision. Commonsense therefore commends the Spartan meritocracy as a sensible worldview. In the quest for understanding, it is clearly superior to the Baroque monarchy.

How does this discussion of worldviews connect to the debate about atheism and theism? And how do the Spartan meritocracy and Baroque monarchy, which may sound like bizarre abstractions, relate to anything in the real world? The questions are answered in the sections below. In the next section, I show that both worldviews have potent manifestations in the world around us and are familiar from our daily lives. In the sections that follow, I show how familiar issues about belief in God relate back to which of the two worldviews we choose to use in search of understanding.

Potent Manifestations

Though they may sound abstract, abstruse and exotic, the two opposite worldviews presented above are in reality familiar parts of our everyday lives. The purpose of this section is to show this. At the same time, it will justify rooting the discussion of belief about God in a debate about worldviews, showing that the approach is of real relevance to what we experience daily. Lastly, by tying the Spartan meritocracy and Baroque monarchy to familiarities, I hope also to make the central argument from superiority of worldviews to atheism's superiority over theism, easier to follow.

The most potent manifestation of the Baroque monarchy is classical religion. For instances, Christians' Baroque assumptions include the existence of God, of the Devil, of angels, heaven, hell, possibly purgatory, and so on; that there is Good and Evil, that there are sins and blessings; that there are reasons why, and much more. Jews may have no devil, but not all their angels do good; they have no hell, but a place of purification; and there are various other differences. Muslims have their different set of core beliefs, Hindus theirs, and so on.

Moreover, the assumptions just mentioned are monarchic, unquestionable generally on pain of heresy, sin, damnation, torture, or some combination thereof. Catholics must learn creed and catechism.

The Roman Pontiff ..., when, exercising the office of pastor and teacher of all Christians, he defines ... a doctrine concerning faith and morals to be held by the whole Church, ... is possessed of that infallibility with which the Divine Redeemer wished His Church to be endowed ... and therefore such definitions of the Roman Pontiff are irreformable of themselves, and not from the consent of the Church.[2]

Admittedly, the doctrine of infallibility was instituted in the late nineteenth century, one of Catholicism's most vehemently anti-intellectual periods. Yet the hubris of the institution haunts its history and lives on monarchic in its current dictates. Likewise, Jews must recite daily the thirteen Articles of Faith which begin with God's existence and attributes. Their author, Maimonides, widely regarded as the greatest Jewish scholar after the fall of the Second Temple, accepted that, like Job, we will want to ask questions. He encouraged the asking, but issued a caveat on answering, especially the biggest questions, such as the existence of God: if you cannot reach the conclusions of the Bible or its great exponents, then, at the end of the day, you must lay aside your misgivings and believe. And religions besides Catholicism and Judaism can be added to the list.

That religions truly are Baroque and monarchic gains strong support from the ways in which they like to portray themselves. Ministers speak of God's will, divine wishes, holy law, and so on, calling them the immutable truth, the unchanging word. In claiming already to know the whole truth or a substantial part of it, in claiming that followers need only accept their authority or the authority of doctrine, ministers clearly advertise both the Baroqueness and the monarchical nature of their creed.

Of course, if the written word of God does not change, the exegesis of his texts often does, with change being compelled from outside, in order for ministers to maintain credence – for no educated person today would heed, say, a sixth century pope. Now, this mutability, indeed, volatility, of God's supposedly eternal truth is significant in the part of the (a)theism debate that deals with how the two theoretical ideals weather the rigours of practice (Chapters 4 and 6). For the present, it suffices to see that religions strive to be and generally are manifestations of Baroque, monarchic principles.

Now let us turn to potent manifestations of the Spartan meritocracy. One might think that, because the Spartan meritocracy is the opposite of the Baroque monarchy, and because atheism is the opposite of theism, that atheism would manifest Spartan, meritocratic principles. However, the relationship between the worldviews and belief about God is not so straightforward, as is made clear in the following sections. Rather, the best known manifestation of Spartan, meritocratic principles is the paradigm of rational enquiry, the system of thought that underlies much of natural science, mathematics, philosophy, and other branches of systematic knowledge. To show that such enquiry is indeed both Spartan and meritocratic, I will discuss some more or less well known incidents from the history of the fields just mentioned. I will begin with a slice of physics, but it is important to note that physics provides a single example of what holds true from algebra to ethics. In using a scientific example at the start, I do not want to imply that all explanation is scientific explanation. This will be obvious in later chapters, but it is best to forestall any 'scientistic' misconstruals.

The meritocratic nature of rational enquiry is clearly apparent in a well known incident from the history of physics, namely Einstein and the ether. Physicists' abandonment of ether illustrates both aspects of the demand that every part of an explanation be productive, that error and otioseness are equally odious. Although most readers will have some familiarity with the concept of ether, I will briefly relate its rise and fall so as to make its methodological moral plain.

Ether entered physics in a thoroughly respectable fashion. Physicists had already developed a detailed and accurate theory of waves and had begun to turn their attention to light. In its essential properties, light was known to be wavelike (in particular, different rays of light could interfere with each other, in a technical sense). So, the natural desire was to explain the nature of light in terms of the current knowledge of waves. To do this, one precondition had to be met. Waves were described, theoretically, in terms of their 'substrate', in terms of the thing that was waving. So, Wordsworth's 'curling waves that break against the shore' 'if the wind breathe soft' are described in terms of the substrate rippling water, and Verlaine's 'longues tones des violons d'autonne', in terms of the substrate vibrating violin strings. Light, apt for description by the theory of waves, must have a substrate, just as Wordsworth's waves and Verlaine's violins had theirs. So, to the substrates, water and strings, was added ether, the substrate of light, through which light waves propagated at a set speed.

The introduction of ether led to an obvious prediction. Imagine bouncing a tennis ball off a wall. If you step forward before catching it, the ball travels less distance than if you step backwards before catching it. So, you predict stepping forward will allow you to catch it that much sooner. Essentially the same experiment could be performed using light for a tennis ball and mirrors for a wall. In the mid-to-late eighteen hundreds several such experiments were performed, originally with the intention of discovering the speed of the earth's movement through the ether. However, none of the experiments produced results consistent with the ball-and-wall model. It was not clear what the source of the error was: it might have been ether, or it might have been a specific technical problem with the experiments.[3] In 1887, Albert Michelson and Edward Morley saw how to avoid this problem and designed an ingenious apparatus consisting of fast spinning arms with mirrors and various slits through which light would pass. If ether was real, then, when a beam of light was split at right angles, sent through the apparatus, and reunited, they would detect a refraction pattern. That is, they would see not a simple beam of light, but a pattern of light and dark stripes. They conducted the experiment twice, three months apart. What they saw was a simple beam. There was no refraction and hence, prima facie, no ether.

Already here one can see the meritocratic mind in action: if ether leads to error, then ether has no place in a search for the truth. However, the story continues, in two stages. First, people sought alternatives to abandoning ether. One possible explanation of the lack of refraction was that the paths that the two half beams of light travelled were in fact equal. If this was so, then, despite appearances, the Michelson-Morley experiment was not like the ball and wall experiment. How could that be? One possibility was that objects' lengths were not constant. Rather, they changed depending on an object's speed and direction of motion in the ether. If that was right, then the difference in the length of the two paths might be compensated for by the change in length of the arms of the apparatus. The exact quantity of the change was calculated in what are now known as the Lorentz-Fitzgerald transformations. Ether could be saved if the transformations were real.

The second stage was Einstein's contribution. He considered two different physicists, developing theories of magnetism, electricity, motion, and so on, in two different laboratories, moving at different speeds. What would the world need to be like if they were to develop essentially identical theories? The crucial assumption here is that the laws of the universe are universal: if Newton's law of gravity, say, applies to apples here, then it applies everywhere, and if not here, then nowhere. What Einstein showed was that from this abstract consideration and two simple assumptions,[4] something very concrete followed, namely, the exact value of the Lorentz-Fitzgerald transformations. The result was the theory of relativity.

The core idea of the ether was otiose, as a broader theory had emerged in which the properties of light could be explained without recourse to substrates. Moreover, the auxiliary notion, that length was independent of motion through the ether, was flat wrong. Both were discarded. So, the story of ether illustrates both aspects of the paradigm of rational enquiry's meritocratic values, not to mention its non-Baroqueness. And it is only one amongst many.

Now, the meritocratic nature of rational enquiry extends even to its Spartan starting assumptions, which are essentially methodological. This willingness to question even the fundamentals proves that rational enquiry is non-monarchic. For instance, Aristotle's science was based primarily on reflection concerning things' essences, that is, on their defining characteristics, and how these could serve as the premises of syllogisms, the engine of his philosophical system. Reflection was more highly prized than experimentation. And, as is well known, this led to the inaccurate cosmology that Copernicus and Galileo criticised at such personal cost. In the search for truth, the outward-looking experimental method supplanted the inner-directed reflective method of Aristotle.[5]

A second example of discarded methodology is Immanuel Kant's notions of intuition and the a priori synthetic. Intended to place science, mathematics, et cetera on metaphysically solid ground, they certainly would have had their place in rational enquiry. However, later writings of Kant indicate that they led him to conclude the then newly hypothesised ether, discussed above, to be a necessary part of human perception of the world. More dramatically, his reflections on intuition, things a priori synthetic, and geometry led him to claim that humans could only conceive of three dimensional Euclidean spaces. While on commission as a land surveyor, the great mathematician Karl Gauss devised possibly the first non-Euclidean geometry. He did not publicise the fact though until a friend requested him to evaluate the significance of his son's discovery of a non-Euclidean geometry. His response was that he had known as much for years – apparently a response he gave often. Kant's system is now a thing of the past.

Even classical logic has been considered ripe for reform in the course of rational enquiry. Mathematicians such as L.E.J. Brouwer urged a revision of mathematics that involved abandoning the law of the excluded middle, formulated by Aristotle as 'There is nothing between asserting and denying'. Philosophers such as Hilary Putnam have argued that quantum mechanics forces on us a 'non-distributive' logic.

Thus, it is clear that rational enquiry, familiar in our everyday lives as science, philosophy, and so on, is a manifestation of Spartan, meritocratic principles, where the meritocracy touches even the most basic starting assumptions concerning how one gains understanding of the world. This example, along with religion as an instance of Baroque, monarchic principles, shows that the worldviews introduced above are not irrelevant abstractions but relate the debate back to issues familiar in our lives. This familiarity shows that a worldview-based debate about atheism and theism is not overly abstract, but is, on the contrary, tightly tied to reality.

Atheism and Theism

But what exactly is the connection between the Spartan meritocracy and the Baroque monarchy, on the one hand, and atheism and theism, on the other? Recall my central claim: whether or not we believe in some kind of deity is dependent on far more fundamental issues, namely, how we go about meeting the seemingly universal human urge to explain, to understand ourselves and world. I have shown the relevance of worldviews in general by arguing that it is by adopting one that we meet this urge. Furthermore, I have shown the opposing Spartan meritocracy and Baroque monarchy to be manifest in the world around us. The key to tying these two worldviews back to the debate about belief in God is the simple realisation, stated earlier, that Spartan, meritocratic principles are clearly superior to Baroque, monarchic ones in satisfying our urge to explain; that only the Spartan meritocracy is plausible and likely to lead to real understanding.

There is no straight and simple correspondence between atheism and theism, and the two worldviews. Below, I will show that some forms of atheism instantiate one worldview, some the other. Likewise, some forms of theism belong to one worldview, and some to the other. However, the Spartan meritocracy does guide one to atheism nonetheless, though not inherently incompatible with theism. The starting point of the discussion is precisely that, how the Spartan meritocracy leads to atheism, not inherently, not by somehow surreptitiously defining God out of the picture, but as a result of the way the world is.

What is centrally important here is that Spartan, meritocratic theories have been proposed in which God plays an active role. That is, there are theories that have argued for God as a theoretical posit, something as necessary to a successful understanding of the world as gravitational forces or subatomic particles. As a way of inducing belief in God, this is entirely in keeping with the Spartan spirit. However, it is a fact about such proposals that they have never worked and it is a fact about God that he has never proved Himself a viable cog, nut, or bolt in any theory of how the world is.

Of course, it cannot be shown exhaustively here that all such attempts are failures, but illustrations can be given. For that purpose, I will discuss a classic example, the work of René Descartes. A more modern attempt by Roger Swinburne features in the following chapter. Many familiar with Descartes' work are likely to remember him from philosophy courses as that French guy who was wrong a lot. But Descartes, despite his errors, was pivotal in our intellectual history, which makes him a particularly good example (and, besides, I will refer back to Descartes occasionally later on). The problems he sought to address were fundamental ones and his answers were revolutionary enough for the Church to threaten public burning of his most famous work, the *Meditations on First Philosophy*. In it, Descartes sought to lay the foundations for the natural sciences and for an understanding of the world generally. As one of the foremost intellects of his day, he was more capable than most to undertake the enterprise.

Descartes' idea, in the *Meditations* and other writings, was that the world was divided into two realms, that it consisted of two 'substances': the physical, and the mental or spiritual. The physical world was to be explained by mechanics, which, for Descartes, meant geometry. One object hitting another object in a fashion describable in geometrical language, producing an effect predictable through geometrical theory: that was the nature of the physical world. In opposition to the physical, there was the mental, spiritual world. This included the mind, which was capable of boundlessly creative activities, such as thought and language. Such activities, Descartes believed, could not be explained, let alone predicted, by brute mechanics. Rather, they involved a completely different substance. The existence of this thinking substance led Descartes to wonder about its nature and those questions led him to conclude that God exists. How he reached that conclusion is not relevant here. The important point is that Descartes did not assume from the outset that God exists. Rather, he believed that a certain methodology, the famous Cartesian scepticism, was forced on anyone seriously concerned to discover the true nature of reality. This led to the realisation that the world is divided into two substances and consideration of one of the substances led, in turn, to the appreciation that God exists. Descartes's method is entirely in keeping with the paradigm of modern rationality: in a universe made spartanly bare by Cartesian scepticism, God played a fundamental explanatory role in nature.

Despite its good pedigree, however, Descartes' theory is incorrect. One objection to Descartes' God is that the arguments used to secure his place in the universe are faulty, as revealed by the discussion in the decades following the publication of *Meditations on First Philosophy*. Though, speaking relatively, that was a minor objection. The deathblow to the Cartesian God was not philosophical, as one might expect, but scientific. It came in the form of Isaac Newton's theory of gravitation, which appeared half a century after Descartes' meditations. Newton showed that the planets' motion obeyed laws not reducible to a geometry of things hitting other things. Planets were certainly physical, yet they refused to obey Descartes' criterion of the physical. Worse still, planetary motion could be explained, but the explanation relied on a mysterious force, gravitation, which acted at a distance, permeating lifeless matter. The only substance that was supposed to permeate matter in any way was spiritual substance. So, not only did the physical not obey the criterion of the physical, it displayed a characteristic of the spiritual.

Newton himself recognised this consequence of his theory of

gravitation. However, a devout man, he had great difficulties reconciling his brilliant intellect with his shadowy dogma and never came to terms with the philosophical implications of his discovery. Instead, he retreated into an obscure and insignificant countryside existence, occupying himself with a hapless search for secret codes in the Bible and by sticking long, thin objects into his eye-sockets. His theory, on the other hand, went on to great things, becoming the mainstay of physical science for the next two centuries and spawning theoretical advances, subdisciplines and technological innovation. Newton's theory enjoying such success, the dichotomous Cartesian universe was doomed and with it disappeared Descartes' pedigree God. Had the world been different, specifically, had physics been mere geometry, then God might have had a place in the universe. Things just have not worked out like that.

The example of Descartes' philosophy, or others like it, illustrates that the paradigm of rationality, though Spartan and meritocratic, is not inherently atheist. It just so happens that every successful theory eschews God, and, within the paradigm, lacking a reason to claim that something exists is reason to claim that something does not exist.

So, we see that the Spartan meritocracy does not commit us to atheism by definition. Rather, it guides us to it as a result of the way the world is. Had the world been otherwise, if, for instance, it had been Cartesian and geometric, a Spartan, meritocratic deity may have found accommodation within it. The next chapter discusses other ways in which such a worldview might make room for God. However, preempting the results, we have been led by the coherent, plausible worldview to atheism, and that is where coherence and plausibility demand we remain.

What of the implausible opposite, the Baroque monarchy? In discussing its manifestations, it became clear that these include major religions. The same holds for newer offshoots, in which a self-appointed or anointed guide, guru, leader pronounces the word of, path to, truth about God. As with the variety of attempts at creating Spartan, meritocratic deities, there can be no exhaustive illustration of all the cases. However, the simple fact is that anyone who professes theistic belief, whether an attenuated spiritualism or a full-blown religious conviction almost certainly subscribes to the Baroque monarchy, a worldview that, by anyone's lights, cannot lead to a correct appreciation of the ways of the world.

Conclusion

We have seen two paradigms: a Spartan meritocracy and a Baroque monarchy. Both are advertised as providing a background for understanding the world, a framework in which to build explanations. However, it is quite clear that only the Spartan meritocracy really makes sense as a worldview. Its alternative is blinkered and shortsighted. This relates the (a)theist question because most forms of theism are manifestations of the Baroque monarchy, whereas the Spartan meritocracy leads, not inevitably, but nonetheless as a fact, to atheism, because of the way the world is. So, once we realise that the universal urge to explain and understand is an admission of ignorance and a dislike of that ignorance, we realise also that only the Spartan meritocracy presents a coherent and plausible end to ignorance, a path to understanding. Furthermore, when we choose between the worldviews, we are led to a decision between atheism and theism. And the superiority of the meritocracy over the monarchy leads to the conclusion that atheism is superior to theism.

Chapter 2

Discovering God

I sought him but found him not – The Song of Songs 3:1

Discovering God

A natural question at this point concerns the possibility that God will be discovered by some successful explanation of the world that has yet to emerge. The atheism thus far defended is only as plausible as the possibility of theism is improbable. In this chapter, I discuss several ways in which God might enter our view of the world. The purpose of this discussion is to shore up the conclusion of Chapter 1, that we are committed to atheism by the principles of the worldview that it makes sense to adopt.

One way for God to enter our view of the world is by proving himself a useful part of a successful theory. That is, a new Descartes might come along and invent a theory with God at its heart. Were such a change in theory to be proposed and accepted, it would constitute so radical a change that it simply defies (my) imagination.[6] Therefore, I have nothing to say concerning it. A more humdrum possibility is that God may enter our world by supplementing some theory similar to the type we have now. In, say, quantum-theory-plus-God, might God be found to be necessary for a full understanding of the world? This seems most unlikely. A brief brush with a book on quantum theory reveals it bristling with mathematics. If our understanding of the quantum universe is to be increased by an increase in entities, then the new entity will have to be mathematical, not mystical. Unless God can solve a mathematical equation, he will do little to improve our understanding of the world. (Whether an appreciation for the

Divine will help us in making sense of our moral, rather than our physical, existence is addressed in later chapters.)

A different way in which we might discover God, an alternative to scrutinising the dark recesses of the universe, is by arguing that His existence follows as a matter of logic from the assumptions of the Spartan meritocracy. This possibility is the opposite to one considered earlier: instead of asking whether the paradigm of rational enquiry is inherently atheistic, we now consider that it might be inherently theistic.

As a Spartan worldview should not assume God's existence as a certainty and should limit itself, as far as possible, to assumptions concerning how one discovers facts about the world, the current alternative suggestion is that God's existence follows as a consequence of the methodological assumptions. So, for example, if we assume some concept of *cause* or *causation*, we can ask what the first cause was and whether it might be God. Or, if we accept that a part of science is the discovery of patterns in nature, then we can ask how those patterns arose. Or, when we see the intricacies of, say, ecosystems, we can ask whether those intricacies should be supposed to result from chance, and, if not, from what they do result. These are, of course, well-known attempts to prove God's existence and represent versions of the Argument from First Cause and the Argument from Design. Other attempts exist, such as the Argument from Ethics, but as these do not rely on the basic concepts and methodology used by scientists, mathematicians, and so on, they are not discussed here. The arguments dealt with now are the Ontological Argument and the two just mentioned.

The Argument from Design

If a brick factory blows up, you don't get a house. Therefore, God exists.

That, in a nutshell, is the Argument from Design. The idea is that houses are complex creations: they have a variety of rooms, each with specific purposes, connecting in various ways. Such complexity could not result from chance, say, from a brick factory blowing up and all the bricks and mortar falling into place. The universe is indescribably more complex than a mere house. It has many more parts involved in much more complex relationships than mere rooms or bricks. So, by the same reasoning, the universe cannot be the result of mere chance. Which means that someone or something must have put it all together: God.

Most arguments for God's existence are like muddy holes: easy to get into, hard to get out of. As a rule, they work by making a subtle mistake and hiding it well. And naturally, finding the rotten apple is much harder than finding the basket that contains it. The rotten apple in this case is the notion of probability. The Argument from Design assumes that we have a firm grasp on the probabilities involved: the probability of houses coming from brick factory explosions versus the probability of human beings, ecosystems, galaxies, et cetera coming from some huge primordial explosion. However, we have not.

A typical university course in probability prefaces the serious mathematics with two titbits to whet the palate: some history concerning the gamblers of ancient Greece and eighteenth century France, and some 'paradoxes', cases in which our intuitions about probabilities are radically wrong. For instance, imagine three dice (blue, green and heliotrope), not numbered simply with 1 to 6, but given more imaginative numberings. So, the blue one might have three 2's and three 4's. If blue beats (on average scores higher than) green and green beats heliotrope, then which one of the blue and the heliotrope wins? Most people reason as follows. If blue beats green, then blue must be the better. Likewise, green is better than heliotrope. So, blue must be better than, and therefore beats, heliotrope. Which is wrong. It is possible for heliotrope to beat blue, as you can prove to yourself by playing around for a quarter of an hour with some dice and some ingenuity. The point for the person teaching the probability course is that intuitions about probability do not reveal the facts about probability. The point for the person considering the Argument from Design is that any argument that relies on intuitions about probability is inherently suspect.

The error in argument is that it pretends that two dissimilar questions are in fact similar. They are: 'What is the probability that a house (or any other complex structure, such as the human eye) could result from a random throwing together of its parts, *given the laws of physics*?'. And: 'What is the probability that the universe, *which includes the laws of physics*, would produce complex structures (such as conscious life)?' The first point to observe here is that these questions are different. The first one makes sense, the second not. A question about probability makes sense when we can characterise, or 'list', all the possible outcomes of a starting situation. So, the starting situation might be an exploding brick factory. The outcomes are all the physically possibly rearrangements of the parts of the brick factory. A house may be one of them, and, if it is, there is a vanishingly small chance that it will result. But the question makes sense, because the laws of physics permit, in principle, a characterisation of the possible outcomes. In the second question, however, there is no such possibility. The task is to characterise all the possible universes, to count them all up, and to see what fraction of them contain complex structures, such as conscious life. However, we simply cannot do that. To begin with, we do not know how many different universes there might have been. To be concrete, assume that there was a Big Bang. Did the Big Bang create the laws of physics? How might they have been different, if so? Could the Big Bang have been different in other respects? These questions are simply unanswerable. The first question seems, in principle, to be answerable, because the laws of physics permit us to characterise the possible outcomes of the explosion. Explosions are after all physical events. But the question ceases to be answerable when the explosion possibly created the laws of physics. We discussed earlier the deathblow of the Newtonian worldview to the Cartesian. We cannot hope to answer, however, what the probability is that the Cartesian 'laws' of physics should have been those which the universe obeyed. We have no reasonable way of ruling it in and no reasonable way of ruling it out. Even if we restrict ourselves to this world with its physical laws, the question is still unanswerable. We would need to know whether the Big Bang could have happened differently but still produce the same laws of physics. Once again, we have no way of listing all the alternatives and of knowing which make sense on paper and in reality and which are merely works of fiction. The problem is that there is just no way to ask the question so that it is both meaningful and answerable, that is, so that it is really a question of probability. And if it is not really a question of probability, then there cannot be a comparison between houses exploding and universes forming. That is, the argument cannot be made.

Probabilities, as remarked, are remarkably tricky things. The probability of a house resulting from an explosion is some teeny-weeny number. But then look at the clothes you are wearing (I assume you are not naked). Think how many atoms they contain. Think how many rearrangements there could be of those atoms that would preserve the outer appearance of what you have on. The probability that you have that arrangement of atoms is a tiny-miny number. But between a teeny-weeny and a tiny-miny number, why should one prompt a belief in God and the other not? Surely, houses are not more divinely inspiring than blouses. Many biologists do seriously wonder about the chances of organic life's existence. Some regard it as probable that there exist monocellular organisms, but find multicellular life amazing. Others draw the line of amazement at sentient life. Others at consciousness. Others at intelligence, insisting that intelligent life must exist elsewhere in the universe. The Argument from Design glosses over complex issues, on which the opinions of experts are divided, meeting them with lay intuitions. In reality, the numbers, the so-called 'probabilities', on which the Argument from Design relies, are not merely spurious. They are meaningless.

One cannot address this topic without mentioning Darwin's theory of evolution, as it undercuts the basis for much of the comparison between houses and human eyes, or houses and ecosystems. A simpleminded challenge to atheism is the question: 'Are you really saying that something as complex as a human eye could be the result of mere chance?' This is meant to make the atheist blush with shame at having notions as preposterous as chance leading to eyes, thus ceding the debate to the theist. What mystifies me about this 'argument' is why anyone makes it. All the way back in 1859, in the introduction to *The Origin of Species*, Darwin asserted that the complexity and variety of life could not result from mere chance. The whole point of his book and of the theory of natural selection was to *explain* complexity and variation, not to fob them off by invoking chance or God. Firstly, then, this common proto-argument misses the point and reveals the ignorance of its professors. Secondly, however, it reveals another flaw in the Argument from Design, at least in some of its versions: that there is a disanalogy between houses and humans or houses and ecosystems. Ecosystems are in their present state not because they suddenly emerged, *ex nihilo*, in their full complexity. They evolved as one part outsmarted, outwitted, outlived, and generally outdid its rivals. The complexity accrued as generations of species fought amongst themselves and against each other. It was not that one minute there was the Big Bang and then suddenly matter cooled and coalesced into ecosystems. Rather, the complex ecosystems built themselves, in a way in which houses, unfortunately, do not. As to the question of whether self-building ecosystems are probable or improbable creatures and what level of complexity we should expect them to attain, these are, as mentioned, real scientific questions. The complexity of the issues defies random assignation of probabilities by enthusiastic theists.

The Argument from Design is incorrect. That much should be clear. However, it has spawned two children, which ought to be mentioned. The first, secret Biblical codes, concerned Newton. The second involves one of the attempts to salvage religion from the battles it loses when it confronts rational enquiry face on. This normally involves saying that religion and science are not in conflict because religious texts already 'contain' all that scientists have discovered, but do so in a non-obvious fashion. Both examples underline the lesson of the Argument from Design, that probability is easily abused and that one should be suspicious of any argument that prestidigitates God from probabilities.

The idea that the Bible encodes secrets between its lines is an old one. Many Jewish scholars have spilled much ink calculating the dual significance that results from using the same symbols as an alphabet and as numerals. This has led to such aphorisms as 'If you take the sharp tongue (*tooth* in Hebrew) away from an evil-doer, he becomes a righteous man'. This 'follows' from interpreting the Hebrew letters used to write *tooth*, *evil-doer*, and *righteous man* as numbers and then observing that the last is the difference of the other two. The computer age has given such 'research' a kick forward. Between 1985 and 1994, a group of mathematicians – Witztum, Rips and Rosenberg – set their computer the kind of task that computers do well and people poorly. The computer was to look for words in the Hebrew text of the Bible, where the letters of the sought word occurred at regular intervals, for example, thirteen other letters between each. The words in the experiment were names and birth or death dates of famous rabbis who had lived long after the Bible's composition. Later experiments revealed that words of similar 'content' often clustered together in passages with a related theme. For instance, various vegetation abounded in passages concerning the Garden of Eden. They then asked themselves what the probability would be of finding the same clusters of words in other texts. The answer, they calculated, was somewhere between a teeny-weeny and a tiny-miny number. Then, invoking amazement at minute numbers, they concluded that the codes that they had cracked evidenced prescient authorship, implying divine inspiration and, hence, God's existence.

The Israeli researchers' work produced a variety of criticisms, not the least of which is that the phrase, 'the Hebrew Bible', implies a fictitious uniqueness. Many different versions of the text exist, some containing letters which others lack. So, what was a code in one version was nonce in another. But the point relevant here is their radical abuse of probability. As mentioned, Arguments from Design proceed by procuring so inscrutably minute a number that, when one recovers from the strain of trying to scrute it, one is compelled to recognise God's handiwork. And, as mentioned, Arguments from Design err in how they procure the number. The error of the Bible code crackers was the question they asked: 'What is the probability of finding the codes we have found in another text?'. It seems quite inevitable that texts will contain words 'encoded' in the fashion that interested the Israeli researchers. I once found an E.E. Cummings poem as replete with encoded body parts as the description of the Garden of Eden is with names of trees. Cummings did not do so on purpose, we can be sure. And, though inspired, his work is not divine. So, finding things that look like codes is not sufficient. Would-be codes must have a meaningfulness that can be interpreted as 'foresight', or 'prophecy', or something similar. So, the real question is: 'What is the probability that any other text, analysed à la Witztum, Rips and Rosenberg, would reveal codes that would strike researchers in late twentieth century as portentous or prophetic or amazing?' Clearly, this is an unanswerable question and the concepts of probability can only be abused in such a context. (Brendan McKay, Dror Bar-Natan, Maya Bar-Hillel and Gil Kalai have recently published an article *Solving the Bible Code Puzzle* in *Statistical Science*, the journal that published the original codes paper. They quote the then editor's interesting introduction: 'our referees ... baffled', the 'paper is ... offered ... as a challenging puzzle'. It is unfortunately unlikely that the challenge met will not receive as much attention as the challenge set by what has become one of the most circulated scientific papers ever.)

Exactly the same error is made by those people who attempt to interpret religious texts in such a way as to make them consistent with modern science. Their aim is to show that the author of the religious text knew the truth all along. A Hindu example of this is Nem Kumar Jain, who sees in the lines 'What does not exist cannot come into existence and what exists cannot be destroyed' (Bhagavad Gita) that the sages of old already knew the law of conservation of matter and energy. Other religions offer other examples. From such unlikely prescience of science, Jain, or his counterpart in other religions, asserts concurrence between Hindu sages and modern scientists too improbable to be mere chance and concludes Hinduism to be divinely inspired. The problem once again is that the probability calculation implicit in the argument is bogus. The probability of Hindu sages and modern scientists concurring is not what is at stake. What is at stake is the probability of someone's finding an *interpretation* of a fragment of text that concurs with something said by scientists. And, as anyone familiar with the exegetical excesses of theism will testify, such 'coincidences' are all but inevitable.[7]

This discussion leads to a conclusion and a caveat. The conclusion is that the Argument from Design is wrong. It relies on seemingly sound inferences based on probabilities. But the probabilities it considers simply do not make sense and often defy analogy. The caveat is: Beware theists bearing probabilities.

The Argument from First Cause

The notion of causation seems indispensable to science. So much scientific work involves hunting for causes. If the idea of causes leads inextricably to God, then the Spartan meritocracy is inherently theistic. The Argument from First Cause has evolved precisely to fill that niche: The world, the argument observes, is full of things causing other things. Something must have set the whole in motion. And that is God.

If the saying is correct that the Devil dwells in the details, then God must inhabit the vaguery. The argument just sketched is scant on rigour. But the argument has an unfortunate feature: what one adds in precision, one subtracts in plausibility. I have spent a good few days asking scientist and philosopher friends about the Argument from First Cause. Naturally, none of the atheists believe it. However, neither do the theists. Moreover, none of them know of a version of the argument that they find compelling and only a few have acquaintances who would give it a second thought.

The problems with the Argument from First Cause emerge when one tries to turn it from a sketch into something solid. The first premise is that everything we observe has a cause. This leads one to wonder what causes causes, and the answer is other causes. Those causes in turn are the effects of still earlier causes. So, what emerges is a huge chain of cause and effect. The Argument from First Cause aims to deduce God from the chain. To do this, the chain is required to come to a stop at some point. That is, the chain must not stretch back forever, and there must be only one chain, not several large chains now tangled together. Assume for the moment that both conditions be met. Then there is a first link in the chain, an uncaused cause, or, perhaps, a self-caused cause. Such a thing would have to be unlike anything we know, and, by paucity of imagination, God must be that thing. Therefore, God exists.

If arbitrariness were a crime, then the inventor of this argument would stand accused on at least four counts. The most grievous confusion on which the argument relies is the first premise. It is not the case that everything we observe has a cause. What is the case, is that everything we observe *seems to have* a cause, or rather, that we interpret the world as being full of causes and effects. However, that is a fact about our interpretation, not about the world. David Hume earned himself a prominent place in intellectual history by arguments to this effect. It is a fact that, in scientific investigation, we assume that events have causes. That is what justifies scientists' search for causes. But that is only a working hypothesis. If it is correct, then that is very interesting. If it is not, then that is interesting too. Either way, the hypothesis that the world divides up into causes and effects, though highly productive, remains merely an hypothesis and one to which the truth of science is no slave. No one has ever proven it, and, very likely, no one ever shall. Even if some very clever person did, problems would still remain.

The argument must somehow convince us that there is only one chain and that it does not go on forever. If there are several or an infinite number of chains, then there may be as many uncaused (self-caused) causes as there are chains. For polytheists, this would be no problem. But for monotheists, it presents the additional burden of proving that there was only one uncaused (self-caused) cause. Even more troubling is the possibility of infinite chains. If chains can continue forever, then there is no first link and, hence, no first cause. These problems seem insoluble. Take the problem of infinity. For a long time, people balked at the idea of the innumerable. In fact, Isaac Newton was criticised by George Berkeley, the Bishop of Cloyne, for using a calculus of infinitesimals in the *Principia*, because 'the infinite belongs to God'. Berkeley's suspicions were more than merely the voice of religious dogma. The infinite had been a vexing topic for some two millennia at that point, ever since Zeno had presented his paradoxes (to step one pace, one must first step half a pace; but to step that distance, one must step half it, too; and half of that must be stepped before; and so on; so how can we ever get anywhere?). And the problems that Berkeley raised were far from trivial, many years passing before they were satisfactorily resolved.[8] In the interim, however, the sheer usefulness of Newton's mathematical discovery largely drowned out philosophical or theological misgivings. Moreover, the taming of infinity got underway in earnest with the work of the great nineteenth-century mathematician, Georg Cantor. Since then, one has learned to live in harmony with the infinite. So, infinite chains of causation may be *prima facie* weird, but that weirdness is non-threatening, and does not even require an infinitely old universe. If the Arguer from First Cause wants to be rid of such chains, then he or she requires strong arguments. Unfortunately, none seem forthcoming and so the argument can only proceed by bluffing.

The uniqueness of the first cause is equally problematic. It is true that much cosmological theorising presupposes or seeks a Big Bang, a single starting point for the universe. However, even the assumption that there was a Big Bang would not be enough for the Argument from First Cause to work. All that would show is that there was an uncaused event that preceded all caused events. It would not prove that all caused events can be traced back, via a huge chain of causal links, to that first event; that there were no other uncaused events later on. In fact, it is hard to see what kind of fact could determine that there was one unique uncaused event, the cause of all events after it. One possibility would be that we find a Theory of Everything that posits a unique uncaused event and has such predictive accuracy that every event anyone ever observed could be deduced from it. So, President Clinton's behaviour with 'that woman' would be a predictable consequence of the Theory of Everything. If that were the case, then we could argue that all events are causal descendants of a unique proto-event. However, such dreams are too far-fetched even for science fiction. The complexity of apparently simple situations defies mathematical analysis and hence prediction. So, the universe, the whole comprising all such intractable parts, is a nut that the hammer of mathematics is far too weak to crack.

Readers can amuse themselves by thinking up other 'facts' that would determine that there was a unique ancestral cause. Yet in all cases, it seems beyond our capacities to discover whether such 'facts' are facts or far-fetched fictions. If there was not a unique uncaused event, then Argument from First Cause is in trouble. The idea of a single cause that begot all other causes conjures up a feeling of awe. That feeling of awe is an environment conducive to introducing God. However, if there are a huge number of such events, even, possibly, an infinite number of them, then they may just represent a fact about our universe: that the working hypothesis, that all events have causes, is incorrect (even if useful). In such a situation, the argument seems less attractive. So, the Arguer from First Cause has a problem, needing, but not finding, an argument that there is a unique first cause.

The plan of the Argument from First Cause is that one shows

first that there was a unique uncaused event and then shows that where there is a unique uncaused event, there is God. The discussion so far has criticised the first stage of the argument. The second stage is equally problematic. On the one hand, there is no justification for the second step. In the best case scenario, the argument would show only that there is a unique uncaused event that caused all other events. Now, if all that one meant by 'God' were 'the unique uncaused event that caused all other events', then the game would be over and the theist would have won. However, God, most theists believe, is much more, possessing omnipotence, omniscience, omniniceness. Some believe that He did more than merely cause the world, He created it, with all the connotations of planning and care that the word 'create' carries. Unfortunately, none of these attributes is deducible from being the unique uncaused event that caused all other events. The main problem is that God is not an event. God is supposed to be an entity and, assuming some naïve difference between the two, entities are not events. All the argument provides, however, is that there was a unique uncaused event. The Arguer from First Cause feels uncomfortable with the notion of an uncaused event but, curiously, feels no discomfort with uncaused entities. But, surely, for every entity, there exists the event of that entity's existing. So, if there is an uncaused entity then there is an uncaused event, namely, the event of the uncaused entity's existing. So, the Argument from First Cause merely replaces one uncaused event with another, which cannot solve the problem.

Suppose that we are simply stuck with an uncaused event or entity. Positing God as our uncaused entity answers no questions about the world and raises the additional question of how God caused the world. The alternative is to leave God out of the picture. This leaves all the questions about the world, but shortens the causal chain and gets rid of questions about how God caused the world. The uncaused entity would then be the world. Recall that the original question was whether the Spartan meritocracy was committed to God, if it assumes a notion of causation. What we see is that the introduction of God introduces new entities and new questions but solves no problems and provides no answers. So, the answer to the original question is that a Spartan meritocracy with causation is not inherently theistic. Indeed, and on the contrary, God, the primer mover, is really a lay-about.

The Ontological Argument

The most venerable of arguments for God, the Ontological Argument is also the most outdated. It aims to squeeze God out of the mere concept of existence and it has a very clear target audience. Think of an area: music, sport, business, beauty pageants. If you would prefer to *be* the greatest in that field, rather than merely to dream of being the greatest, then the Ontological Argument is for you. Define God as the greatest thing there could be. The point just inadvertently agreed to is that something really out there in the world is inherently better than something that just exists in your imagination. If an existing blah is better than an imaginary blah, then existence makes things better. God is defined to be the best thing there is, so, existence must be one of his properties. That is, God exists.

It is not hard to see *that* there is something wrong with the Ontological Argument, but pinpointing the problem is harder. For one thing, it seems that all sorts of other things are ontologically deducible. Existence does not only make good things better, it makes bad things worse. (Think of your worst nightmare coming true instead of remaining a mere nightmare.) So, we can construct an ontological proof of the Devil's existence. Also, we could give an ontological argument that everyone has a 'Mr Right'. Some might object that such variants would abuse the fundamental insight of the Ontological Argument, a problem that more thoughtful formulation of the argument would avoid. To that end, one could create the Ontological Argument for the Ontological Argument to show that there must exist a formulation of the Argument that has only the desired consequences: God, but not Mr Right.

Classical criticism has come in various forms. The most significant was presented by Immanuel Kant. Kant was a man of fastidious regularity, whose strict daily routine never took him more than several miles beyond his native Königsberg (and yet he contrived to be an expert on geography). Though religious, Kant devoted several sections of his magnum opus, *The Critique of Pure Reason*, to discrediting purported proofs of God's existence. His retort is summed up in the well-known dictum: Existence is not a predicate.

Predicates are grammatical entities and it is somewhat amusing to think that God's existence should depend on grammatical taxonomy. Maybe premonition of this conflict led Pope Gregory the Great to reproach a bishop on hearing a report 'which we cannot mention without a blush, that thou expoundest grammar to certain friends'.[9] However, there is sense behind the slogan 'Existence is not a predicate'. When we describe something, we use descriptions, evidently. Kant's point is that '... is red' describes whatever we put in place of '...', but '... exists' does not. To see this, imagine being asked to go on a hunting expedition for a zoo. You are told to seek two animals. An elephant is a large land mammal with tusks and a trunk. An oliphant is a large land mammal with tusks and a trunk and which exists. Two months later you return with a large land mammal with tusks and a trunk. The zoologists' joy on seeing your find soon vanishes as they fall into a dispute about what your find is. Some say that, because it has tusks and a trunk it must be an elephant. The others accept that but observe that the creature also exists, so it must be an oliphant. The first group retorts that of course the thing exists, but that does not make it an oliphant, rather it is existing elephant. And so the argument goes on. The point is that there is no point. Saying that oliphants exist does not add information about oliphants; it adds information about the world, that the latter contains a few of the former. Kant's argument, then, is that descriptions should describe in the sense that they should be lists of predicates. Since '... exists' does not describe '...', it has no place in a description. Hence, to include it in a description of God is to stumble into confusion.

It is not clear whether Kant's argument is correct. There are cases in which attributions and denials of existence do seem to add information, and not only about the world. It is not clear whether or why 'Unicorns do not exist but horses and horns do' should be a fact about the world only and not about unicorns, horses, or horns as well. However, something seems correct in Kant's observation that the problem in the argument lies with the notion of existence. I think the problem can be placed at the door of existence, though I would not do so in Kant's way.

Within the Spartan meritocracy, within mathematics and science, there is a clear practice concerning attribution and denial of existence. If claiming that blah exists is necessary for an understanding of the world, we claim it exists. If not, we do not. In fact, questions of existence rarely really arise as such. They arise as questions of viability of a theory. A prime example of this is the atom. Modern atomic theory began in the nineteenth century as chemistry emerged from its less reputable parent, alchemy. From Mendeleyev until Curie the behaviour of matter revealed itself in ever more concise and beautiful a fashion thanks to the atomic model: rings of negative particles orbiting a core of positive and neutral particles. Yet many leading chemists were deeply dissatisfied with their science, regarding it as a fiction. Even Berthelot, a leading chemist and France's minister of education, insisted that atomic theory not be taught as true but as a useful bookkeeping device. The source of chemists' mistrust of their mainstay stemmed from their belief that chemistry would one day be unified with physics. However, physics dealt with continuous streams of energy, whereas chemistry dealt with chunks of matter. For chemistry to make physical sense, it was thought, it too must use continuous streams as its basic building blocks. Ironically, when the unification of physics and chemistry came, the revolution occurred on physics' side of the fence. Energy ceased to be continuous and streamlike. Instead, it consisted of quanta, tiny chunks studied by quantum physics.

Even before the unification, the extreme usefulness of the atomic model, as well as the accuracy of prediction and precision of understanding that it brought, led to the gradual acceptance of the existence of atoms. It is ironic that, just when physics was ready to live with atoms, a series of experiments showed the traditional model to be incorrect.

The really interesting point is why some chemists felt the urge to deny that atoms existed. The strength of their insistence is indicative of the strength of the will to do what they wanted to prevent: to say that atoms exist. People wanted to say that atoms exist because they were so useful. They would have done so qualmlessly, had it not been for the reduction compunction that chemist-talk be translatable to physicist-talk. The general point is clear: the statement 'blah exists' means, more or less, 'blah is a useful thing to posit in a successful scientific theory'.

Scientists and mathematicians talk of a panoply of entities: atoms, wave functions, imaginary numbers, hormones, neurons, neutrons, and null sets. All these things are said to exist. However, in saying that there exist neurons and that there exist imaginary numbers, does one really say or imply that there is a basic property, existence, which neurons and the square root of minus one share? One does not. Likewise, no concept unites what chairs and tables do with what wave functions do. Certain theoretical entities are said to exist, because they are useful in describing the world at a certain level of abstraction. To speak of existence is to use shorthand. This understood, the Ontological Argument loses its power. We no longer ask whether existence makes God more perfect. Instead, we ask whether being a posit within a successful theory of the world is better than merely being imagined to be such a posit. The question seems too silly to contemplate.

To finish off this section, I would like to advertise a variant of the Ontological Argument that also bases itself on the definition of God as 'that better than which there cannot be'. I call it the None-Too-Logical Argument. From the definition, it follows that nothing is better than God. Also, God must be better than me.

Therefore, nothing is better than me. So, I must be God. Now, I certainly exist. So, God must too. Spotting the flaw is left as an exercise to the reader.

Thus far

Until now I have been making two related points, which, together, comprise one of the central arguments of this book. The first is that there are two ways to respond to the basic human instinct or need to explain the hows and whys of the world. One way assumes that to seek an explanation is to admit one's ignorance and that, if ignorant of the nature of the world, one should make as few assumptions about it as possible. Moreover, all the assumptions one does make should increase one's understanding. That is, they should be essential to one's theory. There may be no useless appendages. This view was named the Spartan meritocracy: 'Spartan' because it makes minimal assumptions and 'meritocracy' because its assumptions and hypotheses survive only on their own merits. The alternative was the Baroque monarchy: 'Baroque' because it begins with an elaborate set of starting assumptions and 'monarchic' because its assumptions are not open to revision and because all attempts to explain observations about the nature of the world must be consistent with, or subservient to, the unrevisable starting assumptions. Most would agree than the Spartan meritocracy is sensible and the Baroque monarchy, nonsensical.

The second point tied the two different worldviews to theism and atheism. Theism associates more or less directly with the Baroque meritocracy. The Credo and Papist dogma, or Maimonides' Thirteen Principles of Faith together with a particular interpretation of the Five Books of Moses, are instances of Baroque assumptions: that the world has a definite origin, life a definite purpose, God a definite nature, and so on. The Spartan meritocracy corresponds only indirectly to atheism. Directly, it corresponds to the paradigm of rational enquiry, that is, the paradigm in which we conduct our science, mathematics, philosophy, and other investigations into the nature of the universe. Such investigation is neither inherently atheistic nor inherently theist. It is not inherent theistic because none of the starting assumptions, such 'Events are caused' or 'The universe is not entirely random but displays regular patterns', force a belief in God. And it is not inherently atheistic because there have been serious scientific and scientific-cum-philosophical proposals, both Spartan and meritocratic, in which God played an explanatory role. It is, however, a fact about the world that no such theory has been true of it. Given how the Spartan meritocracy constructs explanations, atheism follows.

From the first conclusion, that the Spartan meritocracy is sensible but the Baroque monarchy not, together with the association of atheism with the Spartan meritocracy and theism with the Baroque monarchy, a new conclusion follows: atheism is a sensible belief to hold and theism is nonsensical.

Chapter 3

The Price of Knowledge?

For in much wisdom there is much grief ... I commended mirth
– Ecclestiastes 1:19 and 9:15

Theists will, of course, object to the conclusion that atheism is compelled on us by the only coherent worldview, and they will do so in a number of ways. Exploring and exposing some of these ways reveals important aspects of atheism and theism and leads, ultimately, to further appreciation of the superiority of atheism over theism. They form the focus of the following chapters.

On being told that a mature, sensible attempt to understand the world should eschew God, angels, and other bogey-entities, the theist might try just to ignore the argument. The justification would be along pragmatic lines. There may be a disparity favouring atheism on paper, but in practice theism is more conducive to happiness and goodness and, in short, an appreciation of the things that matter in life. Humans are more concerned with ethics than electrons, with laughter than with leptons; more interested in changing circumstances than in universal constants. And, with the former forming the subject matter of science and the latter, a matter addressed by religion, it is in our interest, the theist would reason, to dwell in the comfort of the Baroque monarchy and to shun the minimalism of Sparta's meritocracy. On the face of it, there is something to all this.

But faces are deceptive. In response to this important question, we must now consider the fruits of the two worldviews. It must be conceded, because it is true, that science and religion have very different concerns. But that is only partially relevant.

This is not a contest between science and religion. It is a contest between two worldviews. It may be that the search for human fulfilment has been appropriated by one and largely ignored by the other. Similarly, the quest for knowledge may have been neglected by the former but fostered by the latter. However, the relevant question is what happens when the neglect ceases.

In the following sections, I shall argue that, in this new debate, atheism still emerges as superior to theism. For one thing, rational enquiry has been far more successful at achieving its goal of understanding than theistic dogma has been at achieving its goal of human happiness or fulfilment or righteousness (or however else one may wish to characterise it). Moreover, it is unproductive to apply the principles of a Baroque monarchy to something resembling rational enquiry, though it can be highly productive to apply Spartan, meritocratic ideals to the pursuit of justice, happiness, and fulfilment.

The arguments are arranged so that the boldest claim comes first, that the very method of argumentation in the preceding chapters is inappropriate. This is followed by a not so bold claim, that, for all the superiority of atheism over theism, the Spartan meritocracy is just a theoretical proposal and can be ignored. This disproven, I consider the idea that both worldviews are needed and that, therefore, a compromise is necessary. In less schematic terms, the first argument focuses on the psychology involved in adopting a worldview. The second is a brief and partial catalogue of the successes of enquiry guided by Spartan and meritocratic principles. And the third considers morality, happiness, and so on, asking whether the Baroque monarchy, in the shape of religion or spiritualism, is necessary for fulfilment in these areas. As in the preceding chapters, the facts that bear on these issues range from philosophical and scientific to historical and aesthetic.

Ignoring arguments

A first objection to the conclusion that atheism is superior to theism is that the method of argumentation of the opening chapters is inappropriate to the subject matter. For many people, perhaps most, exposure to theism occurs early in life, when both immune system and intellect are weak and the human organism is prone to interference, with lifelong im- and complications. Consequently, many are raised theists and develop a resistance to later life 'excursion' and many others are raised atheists and develop a resistance to later life conversion. Given that the origin of many (a)theists' (a)theism is second nature from childhood and not the result of reason and reflection, the argument above misses the point. Arguments speak to the head but feelings come from the heart, so to argue about such beliefs is to treat heartburn like headaches. The argument does not address how people come to (a)theism and so it does not address (a)theism.

In the Introduction, I prefaced the discussion by saying that anyone who cared about truth should be an atheist. People who never feel need nor desire to question the beliefs of their upbringing have scant regard for truth. Arguments may well leave such people cold. However, questioning received beliefs is the activity of any responsible, curious individual. Descartes went so far as to believe that failure to do so was a moral error. Furthermore, one of the themes to be explored below is how atheism and theism influence society in terms of justice, welfare, prosperity, etc. Even if one is not interested in which worldview makes better sense *on paper*, there are issues *in practice*, concerning day-to-day life, which are related to the preceding discussion and its consequences. This will become clearer as the discussion progresses.

Ignoring Sparta

Some theists might wish to reject pure reasoning and to opt for a more pragmatic approach to adopting a worldview. The reasoning for this being that, firstly, pure reasoning leads to the conclusion, unsavoury for them, that atheism makes sense whereas theism does not. Secondly, the two alternatives on offer appear to be the Spartan meritocracy, atheism, and an emphasis on rational enquiry, as against the Baroque monarchy, theism, and an emphasis on human needs. Given that the latter is more likely to make for a happy life than its barren competitor, one should just bunk the reasoning and head for happiness.

In this section, I present the first reason why one cannot do this: that the paradigm of rational enquiry is too great a success for it to be bunkable. In later sections, I will illustrate the converse, that the theistic pursuit of the good life is too ignominious a failure for it to be bunkable-in-deference-to.

It would be one thing to abandon the paradigm of rational enquiry if it were merely a proposal on paper. However, centuries of effort have made it much more: it is the most successful attempt to understand the world that the world has ever seen. By dint of breadth, the paradigm stands out. Through the sum total of its theories, it covers more facts, explains more phenomena, and unmasks the mechanisms of more one-time mysteries than any alternative. Such theories are far more than dull catalogues of common things. They are concise statements based on observation that make predictions about situations unknown to the people who created them. They are minute mathematical oracles. Predictions prove that the paradigm reveals truths about the world and as such cannot be dismissed. A related though independent point concerns technology. Technology is the child of science. As scientific understanding of the world becomes deeper and broader, so technology bounds faster and further, assisted by need and aided by accident. Our capacity to manipulate the world through science shows that the paradigm of rational enquiry cannot be written off. Humans try to understand the world. The Spartan meritocracy succeeds.

The discussion will focus on science, but do not lose sight of the point that the success of science is the success of the paradigm of which it is part. Many of the points made below can be translated to mathematics and, to a certain extent, to philosophy. Those points are that rational enquiry transcends the culture and age in which it is conducted, as is to be expected of an investigation into the objective world common to all cultures in all ages; that the successes of rational enquiry are too overwhelming to be ignored; and that technology permits us to interact with the world in a way that can only be possible if the science that underlies the technology has its finger on the pulse of Nature. That is, four themes are highlighted below: theories' objectivity, their breadth of cover, their predictive power, and their offshoot, technology.

Science is an international enterprise, both currently and historically. Today's scientific community includes individuals from almost everywhere in the world. In my department at the Massachusetts Institute of Technology, for instance, there are several people from each of the inhabited continents. The truths unearthed by science are universal truths, transcending individual cultures.[10] Furthermore, the intellectual revolution that led to the birth of modern science was not a solely European affair, even though it did occur in Europe. Whilst Europe wallowed in the Dark Ages, scientific endeavour was fostered by the Islamic world, then in its Golden Age. It, in turn, had received science, via Alexandria, from the ancient Greeks, who, in turn, had built on the knowledge of the Egyptians, the Babylonians, the Chinese, the Hindus, and others. The truly international nature of science suggests that it deals in a currency that does not devalue over time and has the same worth in any culture open to it.

A curious feature of the international character of rational enquiry is that researchers frequently converge on a conclusion, despite coming to it from different directions in different fields. Perhaps the most famous example of this occurred in mathematics. Isaac Newton and Gottfried Leibniz simultaneously discovered the famous calculus of infinitesimals, for which a good proportion of adolescents have never quite forgiven them. Current scholarly opinion is that Newton's discovery predated Leibniz's, though the latter published before the former. What is not so widely known is that seven or so thousand miles and a few infinitesimals away, the great Japanese mathematician, Kowa Seki, was using slightly different methods to reach the same conclusion. The timing of his work is all the more remarkable when one considers that Japan was then cut off from the world under the isolationist, xenophobic Tokugawa Shogunate. Moreover, the discovery of calculus put flesh onto the bones of an insight of Archimedes, which had enabled him to calculate the volumes of various shapes, including the humble sphere (an insight independently achieved by the same Seki).

By claiming that science is culture-independent, I do not want to suggest that science sits in a social vacuum, disconnected from the social circumstances of its investigators. One obvious example to the contrary is that, in periods of war, when there is a need for military superiority, the science of poisons, explosives, and so on advances. Likewise, when especially threatening or dreadful diseases rage, they become the topic of work.

In contrast to necessities spawning invention, political or social ideology sometimes searches for justification in nature. A recent example of this concerns animal homosexuality. Bruce Bagemihl, in *Biological Exuberance: Animal Homosexuality and Natural Diversity* (St Martin's Press, New York, 1999), presents two interesting bodies of facts: evidence of animal homosexuality, and bio- and zoologists' reaction to it. Valerius Geist is unusual in his candour: 'I still cringe at the memory of seeing old D-ram mount S-ram repeatedly. To conceive of those magnificent beasts as "queers". Oh God!' Many, including Geist, have tried to explain away such behaviour, invoking aggression, dominance, mistaken identity, and other non-sexual causes. However, realising this to be 'drivel', Geist, after two years, 'called a spade a spade and admitted that the rams lived in an essentially homosexual society'. Homosexuality has long been regarded in the West as the unnatural proclivity of certain perverted humans. This prejudice influenced both the questions scientists sought to answer concerning animal sexuality and the explanations they constructed concerning it.

The social aspect of scientific work is interesting and important. However, does it undermine the supposed objectivity of science? Does it make science culture-dependent? I think not. For one thing, the employment of scientific results, in the shape of medicines, bombs, and bridges are, for better or worse, culture-transcendent. An epidemic contained or a city destroyed is just that. Furthermore, scientists are people. One enjoys working with friends on related topics. An issue becomes fashionable for a while and progress is made. A theory becomes current for a period and is then cast aside as its shortcomings undermine confidence in it. So, scientific growth is much like organic growth: a seasonal affair, occurring in spurts and stops. It would be a mistake, however, to say that, because the choice of question is under the influence of society's needs and ideals, so must the results of the research also be.

The culture-independent, epoch-independent nature of rational enquiry is important. If scientists are grappling with the world as it really is, then the fruits of their endeavours should resemble one another insofar as they are accurate. Culture and epoch may vary, yet the results of rational enquiry do not co-vary with them. Of course, intellectual, financial, and technological resources affect the questions we may attempt to answer. Archimedes, without our intellectual history, would not think to ask the questions that trouble or torment quantum physicists. Even if he did, he could not conduct any relevant experiments, because he would lack funds and the ability to construct the necessary apparatus. But, when such resources are held more or less constant, independent researches converge. The convergence suggests that the results of the research rely on what we all share: the universe around us. For anyone who cares about truth, this objectivity makes the rational enquiry too valuable to be ignored.

Theories express concisely what we know about the world. Lists express the same explicitly. When sciences are young, the body of facts is obese and concise theories are few. As research unravels the threads, what appeared to be single instances of many facts are revealed as many instances of a single fact. The progress of science consists to a large extent in the abolition of lists. That rational enquiry is able to achieve this is another reason that it cannot be ignored. A prime example of this is Newton's theory of gravitation.[11]

The Babylonians and Egyptians, under pressure of religious obligations, undertook a systematic charting of the movements of stars and planets. As mastery of the skies permitted mastery of the seas in the form of navigation, that knowledge received the dual endorsement of religious devotion and mercantile ambition. As such, it was encouraged and grew in precision and detail. Besides the technological advantage of navigation, astronomy led to the prediction of eclipses. By observing that eclipses were not random events, ancient astronomers could extrapolate and predict when later ones would occur.

The precision of astronomical knowledge increased over the centuries at varying paces and places. When Galileo Galilei turned his attention and telescope skywards, astronomy took another leap forward. The telescope was a remarkably useful invention, which permitted cargo ships to spot and avoid pirates before the pirates even knew they were there. It thus contributed to the wealth and security of Padua, where Galileo worked, and Venice, which ruled it. Galileo's use of the telescope was less worldly. Through it, he observed the phases of Venus and sunrise on the lunar landscape. These discoveries led him to affirm Copernicus' heliocentric theory in the *Dialogue Concerning the Two Chief World Systems*.

It is well known that Galileo's endorsement of Copernicanism, sixteen years after the Church had forbidden it, led to his condemnation by the Inquisition in 1633. However, in light of Vatican documents, long held secret, it appears that the charges were somewhat trumped up.[12] In reality, the Church objected to Galileo's atomism, which could not be reconciled with transubstantiation, the doctrine at the heart of the sacrament of the Eucharist. The political scandal likely to have ensued on charging a man of Galileo's stature with the potentially capital crime of heresy persuaded Church authorities to seek a lesser charge against him. Interdictions and dangers notwithstanding, Galileo continued to expand the corpus of human knowledge. In

1983, in a rare moment of papal perspicuity, Galileo was pardoned.

So, the stock of astronomical observations grew over millennia and, by extrapolating from previous observations, one could predict what would be seen in which place when. The accuracy of such prediction reached its apogee under the auspices of Johann Kepler, assistant to the Danish astronomer, Tycho Brahe. Years of careful observations and reams of mathematical meticulousness led Kepler to three generalisations. The first was that planets move in ellipses around the sun. (Copernicus, an early proponent of heliocentric cosmology, had thought that they should move in circles.) The second specified how the planets' speeds depend on how near they are to the sun. And the last generalisation connects distance from the sun to the time taken to complete one orbit.

Kepler's advances were highly significant. However, the real mystery had not been solved: regularities had been discovered, but their cause remained a mystery. One theory was that angels were charged with pushing the planets. The mystery finally relented to the genius of Newton. Combining ancient Greek mathematics with a force called 'gravity', Newton found that all motion of the planets was reducible to a Spartan set of posits, each of which merited its place in his theory. In a supreme moment of synthesis, he had produced a theory that abolished the need for the long lists astute and conscientious priests had begun thousands of years earlier.

Newton's theory, and its advance over the lists of facts that preceded it, provides only one of many possible examples of the breadth of cover a good theory offers. The true breadth of Newton's theory is astounding. Kepler's three distinct observations were consequences of it, as were Galileo's observation that objects near the earth's surface fall sixteen feet in a second, why there are tides, and why two a day. Such cover is testimony to the efficacy of the methods of science and, so, to the paradigm of rational enquiry.

Two related points follow neatly on from the discussion of

Newton's law of gravitation. The first concerns the predictive capacity of a theory and the second, its capacity to be implemented in new technologies. Both of these underline the point of this section: that the fruits of the paradigm of rational enquiry are too remarkable for one to be able to dismiss the paradigm and the worldview to which it belongs.

The Danes of the seventeenth century were great astronomers. Into the company of the two already mentioned, Brahe and Kepler, I want to introduce a third: Olaus Roemer. Observing Jupiter and its satellites, he noticed that they did not appear in the right place at the right time. Lateness and earliness averaged out, the results predicted by Newton's theory were right, but when near the earth, the moons were early, and when distant, late. In such situations, one can doubt three things: the observations and calculations, the theoretical assumptions, or that one has all the pieces of the puzzle. Roemer was sure of the first two and had faith in Newton's law of gravitation. So, he was forced to search for the missing piece. Roemer proposed that what was missing from his calculations was how long it took the light that he saw through the telescope to travel from Jupiter and its moons to his retinas. From this, he was able to determine the speed of light.

Newton's law continued to illuminate the heavens. At the beginning of the nineteenth century, Uranus was the most distant planet known. (This was long after the death of Newton, and even longer after that of the assertion that an adequate theory of cosmology must explain why only six planets could orbit our sun.) However, it did not follow the (near) elliptical trail that Newton had blazed for it. Careful calculations revealed that its divergence would be exactly those we would expect if there were an eighth planet following a particular orbit. The results derived on paper were borne out by the telescope and Neptune entered the celestial map. The prediction, or deduction, that there is an eighth planet was made approximately simultaneously by John Couch Adams and Urbain Leverrier, illustrating again how independent researches under like circumstances converge.

The story of Edmond Halley illustrates the predictive power of good theory and signposts a topic discussed below. From the work of Kepler and Newton, Halley predicted that a certain comet would return in seventy-six years' time. Indeed, he calculated to the minute the time at which it would be seen at a certain point in the sky. Such precise calculation was prompted by social circumstance. Halley was part of an intellectual battle, part of the larger war between 'explanation' and explanation, the former being a subdiscipline of theology and the latter, a part of science. On the one hand, science wanted to claim that comets were heavenly bodies like any other, obedient to laws such as Newton's. On the other, the Church wished to maintain that comets were fireballs thrown at the world by a God indignant at our iniquities. Believers denounced their opponents as 'calves gaping at the barn door'.[13] Indeed, until the end of the seventeenth century, professors of astronomy were obliged to swear not to teach that physical laws control comets. In the end, science won and the comet, which returned as predicted, now bears its discoverer's name. Such conflicts between science and religion reveal much about the efficacy of the systems from which they spring. The topic is discussed more below.

Good science, besides increasing our knowledge of the world, often allows us to manipulate the world in new ways. That is, science leads to technology and technology changes our lives and our world. It is somewhat disappointing that Newton's law of gravitation, so beautiful in its simplicity and so far-reaching in its consequences, should provide such a poor illustration of the point I want to make. It has had some practical application. For one thing, getting a man onto the moon would have been near impossible without it. But, though an application, it probably was not terribly practical. More practical is our ability to send satellites into orbit. Much of the modern lifestyle revolves around things that revolve around us. Communications systems are one example of such satellite-dependent, Newton-dependent technology. Geoprospecting and tide predictions are practical applications of the law of gravitation. And astrologists, knowing the positions of the planets, are able to make more precisely inaccurate predictions – a not-so-practical application.

There is, however, a relative of Newton's discovery that excellently illustrates how science permits us to manipulate the world. Our mastery of electricity has transformed our lives. If theories of global warming are correct, electricity, or our production of it, has also 'helped' to transform the world. Our daily comforts, such as night-time light and hot water, as well as our ability to save lives with dialysis machines (and end them with electric chairs, if one lives in such primitive places as Texas), all depend on electricity. The theory of electricity was developed by a series of great minds – Faraday, Coulomb, Favart – culminating in Maxwell, whose work is so beautiful mathematically that, when an undergraduate studying mathematics, I was advised to read it ignoring the physics. It is related to Newton's law in that both are 'inverse square laws', a name based on their mathematical representation. It is an abiding mystery as to why the universe should have two laws that are so different but look so similar. No one has yet succeeded in making these similar laws two sides of the same coin. Electricity is a prime case where our mastery of science has led to new ways to influence our environment.

The electrification of daily life constitutes technological progress. Science aims to understand the world. Technology, the implementation of science, aims to manipulate the world. No one can deny that technology has transformed our lives and our interaction with the world and that it continues to do so. The edifice of technology would be impossible without the foundations of science. As the base of scientific knowledge increases, technology progresses and expands with it. Technology is the dependent of science and one cannot recognise the reality of the former without admitting the efficacy of the latter.

Conclusion

This section began with the goal of rebutting half of an argument. The argument was that one should ignore the conclusion of the first sections of this book. It may be that the Spartan meritocracy is conceptually superior to the Baroque monarchy. However, the argument runs, the Baroque monarchy is more in tune with what humans need in order to lead a happy, fulfilling existence. So, the Spartan meritocracy, for all its theoretical pedigree, is not a viable worldview for our day-to-day lives. It can just be dismissed. The first half of my response to this view was that the Spartan meritocracy cannot be dismissed for the simple reason that it is too successful. This section has been a catalogue of those successes. The point of the section can be summarised in a simple question. If the methods and principles of the Spartan meritocracy are wrong or awry, how have they been able to unearth so many facts, to give them such concise and objective expression, and to put them to so many uses?

Keats' objection

The view I am pursuing throughout this book is, as mentioned earlier, in the spirit of the Enlightenment. The Enlightenment had many enemies. Many, especially amongst the Romantics, would find the objection just outlined quite to the point. One such was John Keats. He often explores, or expounds, the idea that emotion and beauty are paths to Truth. A true Romantic, he loathed the analytical, anti-emotional mania of the Enlightenment's followers. The following extract from *Lamia* illustrates his view.

> ... Do not all charms fly
> At the mere touch of cold philosophy?
> There was once an awful rainbow in heaven:
> We know her woof, her texture; she is given
> In the dull catalogue of common things.
> Philosophy will clip an Angel's wings,
> Conquer all mysteries by rule and line,
> Empty the haunted air, and gnomèd mine –
> Unweave a rainbow ...

The poem tells the tale of a serpent, disguised as a beautiful, manipulative woman, who has tricked a handsome nobleman of Corinth into marrying her. However, she is unmasked at the wedding banquet by a wise, wizened philosopher, the tutor of her betrothed. Found out, she vanishes and the young man, broken-hearted, dies. The end is meant to illustrate how awful the results of a life ruled by Philosophy are.

I have shown above that the Spartan meritocracy is a successful worldview because it reveals the truth about the world. However, Keats can still object that we are better off under the Baroque monarchy and free from Sparta's meritocracy. To make his point, he could cite two sets of facts. Firstly, 'Philosophy will clip an angel's wings, unweave a rainbow'. That is, rational enquiry reduces to numbers and formulae the beauty of rainbows and our wonder at the other items in what he ironically calls 'the dull catalogue of common things'. Goethe would agree with him on this point. He criticised Moses Mendelssohn, an important Enlightenment figure, by saying that once he, Mendelssohn, pinned the butterfly into his catalogue, he turned it from a beautiful, bright creature into a dull and lifeless corpse. The analytical aims of rational enquiry are irreconcilable with our appreciation of beauty, and an appreciation of beauty is fundamental to the human soul. The choice, then, is between analysis and happiness.

Presenting Keats' opinion, I quoted from *Lamia*. Ironically, the response to Keats is another quotation from the very same poem. In one of their love scenes, the Corinthian youth tries to raise his serpent lover's spirits. His beautiful speech begins:

> 'My silver planet, both of even and morn!
> Why will you plead yourself so sad forlorn ...

The irony here is what Keats compares his serpent lady to: the planet Venus, which shines in the morning and the evening. The ancients believed that what they saw in the morning was a star, not a planet, and that it was different from the star they saw in the evening. It was a major discovery that the 'morning star' and the 'evening star' are in fact planets and the same one at that. Surely, such a discovery had 'empty[ied] the haunted air', was a mystery 'conquer[ed] ... by line and rule', and had interred two heavenly bodies into 'the dull catalogue of common things'. And yet, Keats found the steadfast, radiant Venus a worthy object of comparison for his heroine. Charm had not flown 'at the mere touch of cold philosophy'.

Keats' worry that science destroys beauty is understandable but wrong. For one thing, examples such as Newton's law underline the beauty and majesty of the world. To find that the whole solar system dances to the same music must fill anyone with awe. Scientists are people who have never got over the miracle of Jesus and the hungry masses. From the tiny amount of bread and fish, there came food enough for many. In science, we are always in pursuit of that miracle. Newton is one person who found it. From one equation follows the movement of tides, comets and planets.

Secondly, as Keats' comparison of the serpent lady with Venus illustrates, scientific discoveries do not bleed the imagination. They feed it. The same is more emphatically true for technology. As advancing chemistry catalogued dull things, new compounds and new colours could be created. The painter's palate grew along with technology. Art expanded with science. Photography and film became vehicles for artists. Keats is right: science has denuded the world of many mysteries. But, what it took away in mysteries, it has repaid in beauty, and that, after all, was Keats' main concern.

Suffering from acute tuberculosis, untreatable by medical science, Keats must have found greater solace in Art than in Philosophy. Yet, if he could see the world now, I doubt he would regard science as the enemy of beauty and art as its defender. The strangest things pass for art nowadays: recent entries for the Turner prize include film footage of policemen trying to sit perfectly still for unreasonable lengths of time, and famous films slowed down to the point of incoherence. Compare those efforts with the fractal intricacies of Mandelbrot sets[14] or with photographs of distant galaxies. Compare some modern music with sonar recordings of whales or dolphins. In such cases, science, not art, seems to be the guardian of beauty. If he could have known, Keats might have held a different opinion.

A second argument that we might be better off without the Spartan meritocracy, even accepting its efficacy, can be made on the basis of technology. Suppose one accepts the argument that our technological success is indicative of our scientific success and so proves that the Spartan worldview reveals universal truths. One can still point to all the horrors that technology has produced: atom bombs, germ warfare, poison gases. The world would have been a better place without these, and so, without them and their cohorts, we would find ourselves in a possibly poorer but a purer place. However, from that it does not follow that the world would have been better off without the technology and the science that led to atoms bombs and so on. And it certainly does not follow that we would have been better off without science and technology altogether.

Science gives us knowledge and technology gives us know-how. Yet nothing in the Spartan meritocracy obliges us to build atom bombs and to drop them on our enemies, nor to pump poison gases into chambers or across battlefields. It may tell us what the best way is, given our technological situation, to wipe out our enemies. But it does not tell us that wiping out our enemies is something we should be engaged in. Ingenious insights require ingenious minds, just as evil implementations require perverted minds. When technology is employed for evil, that evil is a reflection of the implementer, not of the technology they abuse.

The science and the technology needed to build atom bombs are part and parcel of the science and technology we use to treat cancer. To lose one is to lose the other. Germ warfare can be the search for weapons against enemy germs just as much as the search for germ weapons against enemies. Understanding one is part of understanding the other. When one undertakes a research project, there is no way to tell in advance whether its results will do good or evil. The Internet, originally developed for secure wartime communication, looks set to build bridges between people across the world. By contrast, Godfrey Harold Hardy, the great British number theoretician and ardent pacifist, prided himself that his work on huge prime numbers had no practical application and so could not harm humans. He would turn in his grave if he knew that his mathematics serve as the basis for encryption of military secrets.

The point is that technology's abuses are the fault of the abusers and not of the technology. A car can run someone to hospital and save their life, and it can run someone over and kill them. The former does not make cars inherently good and the latter does not make them inherently bad. And that is generally the case with technology. To dismiss the whole of technology, the whole of the Spartan meritocracy, because of technology's abusers, is to throw out the baby with the bath water, and the bathtub and the towels too. It is a move that would reintroduce epidemics, increase infant mortality, decrease longevity and revive needless suffering. In other words, it is a non-starter.

Conclusion

This chapter has considered the possibility of ignoring the argument of the first chapters, that the Spartan meritocracy, which leads to atheism, is the most sensible worldview. The first idea was that, because the worldview is merely a proposal on paper supported by theoretical considerations, it can be ignored. By illustrating four successes of Spartan, meritocratic enquiry, namely objectivity, breadth, predictive capacity and implementability, I argued that ignoring it was not possible. The second idea, Keats' objection, is not that we *can* ignore Sparta, but that we *should*, because the rigours of such enquiry are the exact opposite of what the human spirit needs for fulfilment. I calmed this qualm by indicating that it relies on an understandable but incorrect analysis of the facts. The conclusion is, then, that the Spartan meritocracy cannot be ignored.

Chapter 4

Contra Compromise

Nay but we will have a king over us – Samuel I 8:19

I have been defending the Spartan meritocracy on two counts: that its successes are, firstly, too great to be dismissed and, secondly, too useful to be disregarded. However, this still does not tell us whether the Baroque monarchy is indispensable to a happy, meaningful existence. Are we forced to live with two fundamentally incompatible worldviews? This new possibility is one of compromise, less bold than the claim considered and discounted in the previous chapter, that we can or should alto-gether ignore the Spartan meritocracy and its theoretical superiority. If we were forced to accept the Baroque monarchy as essential to human wellbeing, then there would no longer be any grounds for criticising theism. I am, therefore, going to argue that the Baroque monarchy is not essential and that, in fact, we are better off without it.

What about love?

As indicated at the outset, this book grew out of discussions with friends. It has happened more than once that I would outline why the Spartan meritocracy is superior to the Baroque monarchy and why that indicates that atheism is superior to theism and that I would be met by a particular type of response. The simplest version of it is: 'What about love?' People generally intend this question in one of two ways: a silly or a sensible.

The silly way does nothing more than point out that there is something that science has been unable to explain. As a working scientist, I am always baffled as to why people bother to tell me that. If anyone knows that science has not explained everything, it is the working scientist: our jobs depend on the incompleteness of science. Besides, people who put that 'argument' are playing a gamble where the odds are well against them. The past is littered with claims that such-and-such a field lies beyond the grasp of science and such claims have a habit of being wrong. One instance already mentioned was René Descartes' belief that human language was inexplicable. However, forty years after Noam Chomsky's 'cognitive revolution', language has fallen well and truly within the grasp of science. Geology was also thought to be an impossible science. This followed Archbishop Ussher's assertion, based on close textual analysis of the Bible, that the world had begun on Sunday 23 October, 4004 BCE, at the very proper hour of 9:30 – *heure locale*, one assumes. The assertion contradicted the arguments of Wycliffe, now recognised as the father of the geological sciences, who had used fossils and rock structure to argue that the world must be several hundred thousand years old. His blasphemy so enraged the Church that it ordered Wycliffe's bones disinterred, shattered and scattered over the ocean, that they cease to contaminate the earth with dissent. And many others have tried to limit the scope of science on other grounds for a variety of reasons. Picking a topic as inexplicable is a dangerous game. In that shape, the 'What about love?' objection is just wrong.

However, there is another way to interpret the objection: as pointing to the inherent limitations of human reason and, hence, to rational enquiry. Once we establish that the Spartan meritocracy does not provide the answer to all questions, it seems reasonable to look elsewhere for answers. Specifically, Keats would say, we should seek elsewhere answers connecting truth and beauty, beauty and truth, 'all ye know on earth and all ye need to know'[15]. And here, one would turn to religion, or spiritualism, or God – to some manifestation of the Baroque monarchy.

To appreciate the limitations of human reason, step back four centuries in history to the Renaissance and early Enlightenment. Many great thinkers of those times were under the peculiar impression, or dogmatic assumption, that the world, in all of its aspects, was entirely comprehensible to the inquisitive rational mind. All was amenable to reason. The belief may have stemmed from the Bible, which claims that Man was, or men were, the pinnacle of creation, destined to rule as master of the field. This destiny, congenital supremacy with hereditary superiority, may have led men to think their minds capable of understanding everything. However, the influence of the Bible has waned. One no longer thinks things true simply because the Bible says so.

Rats provide an instructive parallel. Rats can be taught how to run certain types of mazes. For instance, if the maze involves alternately turning left and right, then they can learn it. However, some mazes involve different concepts. A numerical maze, for instance, might involve taking one left turn and then two rights, then another left and two more rights, and so on. Rats cannot run numerical mazes. They resort to chance exploration to find the way out. Now, if certain very clever rat-scientists undertook to systematise rats' knowledge of mazes, they would conclude that there are, say, two types of mazes: alternating and non-alternating. Only alternating mazes, they would say, have any structure. Non-alternating mazes are chaotic. However, their conclusion would only be partially an objective theory of the world. Their theory would reflect the interaction of the structure of the world with the structure of their consciousness or mental resources.

We are rats in a maze. Our mental powers are part of our biological endowment, just as are our having two arms, on average, and our being unable to see infrared and ultraviolet light. Our science is rat-science. The questions we ask and the answers we give are reflections of our biological limitations and their interaction with the world. That evolution has provided us with science-forming faculties is amazing in its own right. However, to claim that there are no questions that our minds are unable to raise and to claim that we can find answers to all the questions we shall ever raise, is to subscribe to an obscure and curious dogma, a principle neither Spartan nor meritocratic.

The human mind has climbed many mountains. However, there are some mountains that mind cannot climb and others that the mind's eye cannot even see. 'What about love?' is a poetic way to point to these innate limitations. The issue is whether anything follows from that correct observation. That is, we must decide whether the incompleteness of the Spartan meritocracy forces us to adopt the Baroque monarchy in one of its guises. To be precise, the question is this: given that there will always be questions we cannot answer, does it make sense to adopt an answer?

The response is an emphatic: no. Consider explicitly what we are being asked to do. Having realised that not everything is sensible within the compass of our understanding, we are being asked to believe things that are insensible within the compass of our understanding. So, suppose for the moment, that love poses one of the questions unanswerable by science. (Not that I understand what that question is meant to be. Is it 'Why is there love?' or is it 'Why is love not more sensible?' or is it 'Why did Caesar love Cleopatra?' or is it something else?) The scientist admits that there is insufficient evidence to give the semblance of a plausible answer. Surely, such a lack of evidence is not meant to justify a belief in God, or the Catholic credo, or the Hindu's belief in karma and reincarnation. The honest admission of ignorance to a sensible question does not justify a pseudo-answer to a silly one.

This point may sound obvious, but the error it uncovers is very common. An oft-aired challenge to atheists is 'Where does the world come from?' or some equally prickly question. And my favourite answer is: 'I give up; but can you tell me how to say salamander in Wompanoag, the language of the Indians who saved the settlers on the *Mayflower*?' – which they cannot because nobody knows what the Wompanoag for salamander was. The point of the first question is that because the atheist has no evidence and therefore no justified answer, the theist's unjustified answer is meant to seem plausible by comparison. This is precisely the nonsense just referred to. Just because there is no answer one is justified in giving, it does not mean one is justified in giving whatever answer one will.

Recall what the point of the whole discussion is. In the first section, I gave an argument that a Spartan, meritocratic world-view is superior to a Baroque, monarchic one and, from that, that atheism is superior to theism. The question at the moment is whether one needs both the meritocracy and the monarchy. Currently, the issue is whether the incompleteness of science, the child of the Spartan meritocracy, forces one to accept that the Baroque monarchy is valid too. And the answer is: no. It is perfectly coherent to start off with Spartan, meritocratic ideals and to end up with Baroque, monarchic ones. That would happen if a version of the Baroque monarchy were the result of an enquiry that begins with sparse assumptions and rigorously justifies all its posits. However, finding that we cannot answer all our questions does not justify the Baroque monarchy. It still remains an improbable method for finding the truth about the world. That the Baroque monarchy is a sensible worldview to subscribe to, is a proposal like any other. Proposals are evaluated for plausibility on the basis of what we know. Only our knowledge can make a proposal plausible. Ignorance, a lack of information, cannot make a view more plausible. So, when the Spartan meritocracy reveals that ignorance is part of the human condition, that ignorance neither detracts from the meritocracy, nor does it support the rival Baroque monarchy.

This last turn in the discussion has drawn us away from the first half of the argument and into the second. That is, we are no longer talking about whether the Spartan meritocracy is too successful and useful to be ignored. We are instead considering whether the Baroque monarchy has merits that force it upon us. We are answering the question of whether there are aspects of human life that can only be fulfilled by adopting some version of the Baroque monarchy. If there are, then the original argument for the superiority of meritocracy over monarchy, and atheism over theism, would be irrelevant, and theism would be justified after all. This section has been a presentation of one version of the argument for the monarchy: one based on the incompleteness of the Spartan worldview. That argument failed. The new question is whether there are better versions.

The happy monarchy

To believe in God is to subscribe to the Baroque monarchy. However, that worldview is questionable and not as sensible as the Spartan meritocracy, of which atheism is a consequence. More familiarly, we see the meritocracy manifested as science and the monarchy as religion, spiritualism, or other forms of theism. Science and religion deal with very different areas of life. Religion deals with justice, with morality, with happiness, and with other issues fundamental to human society and life. Therefore, it seeks to answer questions that traditional natural science ignores. Yet it is impossible for most people to lead a fulfilling life without forming views on justice, morality and so on. So, traditional science cannot meet all our needs and human nature abhors the vacuum that science leaves. Religion, spiritualism, and other forms of theism can fill that gap and, if we are to be balanced beings, it must. Given that our wellbeing and our society's welfare depend on this, we must disregard any merely theoretical argument that atheism is superior to theism.

This is the argument I wish to address. I have already indicated that it must be modified if we are to take it seriously. The debate between atheism and theism does not depend on the debate between science and religion. So, to frame the issue as above, in terms of science and religion, is to miss the mark. The (a)theism question is an issue of worldviews. It is true that religion, a potent manifestation of the Baroque monarchy, has concerned itself with issue, fundamental to human life. It is true that science, a potent manifestation of the Spartan meritocracy, has tended to ignore such issues. However, the real question is whether that is an issue of theory or of practice. Is the Spartan meritocrat destined to ignore such issues? Can they be addressed only by the Baroque monarch?

As before, my answer comes in parts. One part is that the division is not necessary. In fact, it is not even accurate. Thinkers working within the Spartan meritocracy have for a very long time now addressed such issues as the meaning of life, the nature of virtue, and the road to happiness. I shall discuss these issues below. Another part, which I shall discuss immediately, concerns whether the Baroque monarchy has any right to lay sole claim to such topics as meaning, virtue, happiness and so on. To understand what I am getting at here, recall the nature of the position I am responding to. It is a pragmatic one. Disliking the anti-theistic conclusion of my opening argument, the theist claimed that the pragmatic virtues of theism (meaning, virtue, happiness, and so on) outweigh the logical virtues of atheism. So, to see whether there is any substance to the theist's claim, what we need is a pragmatic examination of theism. We need to know whether theism has made life meaningful, whether it has revealed the anatomy of virtue or the geography of happiness.

My answer is that theism has not succeeded in the goals it has set itself. Where it has made life meaningful, it has also made it miserable. It has brought as much hell as happiness and, at times, it has created a vacuum of virtue. In this subject, history is the best teacher. Of course, I do not claim that religion is unequivocally evil, nor anything similar to it. The relationship between religion and goodness is complex. However, close examination of it reveals an important point: that religion has no right to lay claim to virtue, goodness, and their cousins. Having realised that, we can see that the argument I have been concerned to defeat is concertedly defeated.

Before launching into history, I wish to frame it philosophically. Essentially, the objection I am responding to is a series of simple questions: How can you be happy without God? How can you be fulfilled? Now, there is, of course, a very famous version of this type of question and I shall use it to frame the discussion that follows:

How can you be moral without God?

The point of this argument dressed up as a question is not to prove that God exists. It is to prove that one ought to believe He does. If the Argument from First Cause, the Argument from Design and the Ontological Argument are logical arguments for God, then this argument based on ethics is a pragmatic one. Many continue to regard religion, and usually one particular religion, as the only possible foundation of moral life. Such people are inclined to challenge atheists with the question of how one can be moral without God. The answer the theist expects is that one cannot. Were it not for theists and religions, we should very quickly descend into destitution, debauchery and dastardliness.

What always strikes me when I hear the question is how very questionable the questioner's ethics must be. If all that keeps them from murder, theft, torture, and so on is that they have been told not to, then they must be ignoble indeed. Even more so if their motivation is fear of punishment or desire for reward. Personally, I believe in human goodness and nobility. I do not mean that we are inherently good, whatever that would be. Rather, I have seen people behave altruistically and charitably, doing a good turn, at times causing themselves considerable bother, and they do so having no greater goal than to be helpful. The impulse to good exists. We behave morally, altruistically and charitably because we want to. Carrots and sticks do not enter into the equation. Anyone who seriously suggests that one cannot be moral without God must lack such inclinations to good and be inclined only to evil.

Faced with this embarrassment, the theist would concede the point and alter that of the question. We have, the theist would grant, moral intuitions. The point is how. How could we know that robbery is wrong, pilfering pernicious, embezzlement evil? More importantly, why should we feel compelled to act on such knowledge? Such knowledge is too wonderful for any mundane explanation such as that humans are just made like that. So, the theist, by hook or by crook, or by both, concludes that God is the source of such wonderful knowledge and that we have it because He wants us to do good and shun evil.

Arguments for God from ethical intuition have had famous adherents. The most surprising must be Immanuel Kant. His *Critique of Pure Reason*, mentioned above, fairly solidly disposed of the three arguments for God most common at his time: the Ontological and those from Design and First Cause. This might have led many to think Kant an atheist. However, having sabotaged earlier attempts, he provided his own, one based on moral intuition. He declared himself forever fascinated by the starry skies above him and the moral code within him. In short: Wow!, therefore God exists.

Such arguments raise two questions. The first is whether they are correct and the answer is that they are not. In order to work, it must be shown that God is the only plausible explanation of the origin and nature of our moral intuitions. This tactic, arguing for God by excluding all other possibilities, is risky because other possibilities often crop up later. All that is needed to undo the argument then is for the whiff of plausibility to attach to an alternative explanation, a more mundane one, eschewing the elaborateness of God and his minions. Precisely that has been happening for the past hundred and something years.

The key to the argument is the human mind, how it learns and how it grows. The first major contribution was Sigmund Freud's. Freud's specific proposals were largely a product of the slice of history and layer of society in which he found himself. However, his broad ideas – that adults' dispositions are products of their childhood – passed the litmus test of great scientific insight: the Catholic Church denounced them as contrary to its teaching. Noam Chomsky's work suggests an interesting way to implement Freud's insight into a working scientific theory, which I shall briefly discuss. In the late 1950's, Chomsky proposed that children are good at learning languages and adults are good at using them because those abilities are part of our biological endowment, just as being a biped is. Now, linguistic knowledge is similar to moral intuition in several respects.

Firstly, there is a remarkable consensus in judgments in ethics and linguistics, even though people do not know what criteria they base their judgments on. For example, suppose you are driving a tram and a technical error occurs. Unable to stop the tram, you can either continue on your current track, which would cause the deaths of five workmen whose pneumatic drills prevent them hearing the tram, or you can turn onto a side track, which would cause the death of one workman working under the same conditions. Everyone agrees the moral thing is to turn and kill one person: to do nothing would be wrong. However, pretend now you are a doctor with five patients all of whom will die within hours if they do not receive various transplant organs. By chance, a man, without family or friends wanders into your office and you realise that he has all the organs the others need and that he is a suitable donor for them all. Your choice is between doing nothing, which would cause the deaths of five people, and drugging and butchering the man, which would cause one death in preventing five. Again, judgments are unanimously not to kill the man: to do nothing would be right. Yet, there is no obvious difference between the situations. Both are choices between inactivity and five deaths, and activity and one. Yet our judgments are different and we do not know why.

Linguistic intuitions are the same. We all know it is grammatical to say *I need to fix the fridge* and *I need a man who can fix the fridge* and *I need a man who can fix the fridge with a spanner*. However, they do not all form grammatical questions if one deletes *the fridge* in the first two (*with a spanner* in the last) and place *What do* (*How do*) at the start. So, *What do I need to fix?* is fine. But *What do I need a man who can fix?* – answer *the fridge* – is quite bad. And *How do I need a man who can fix the fridge?* – answer *with a spanner* – is just ludicrous. Although we nearly all agree on these facts, almost none of us has ever stopped to consider what makes one grammatical, another ungrammatical, and the third practically unintelligible. As with the tram, the intuitions are clear, the criterion opaque.

A second similarity is that linguistic and moral dispositions tend to be homogeneous across homogeneous social groups. So, children who spend much time together tend to talk, and think, alike. They are relatively similar to their siblings, less so to their parents. And thousands of miles away, people speak differently and have quite different opinions about what is moral and what not. Linguistic and ethical likeness co-vary with general cultural likeness. A third similarity is that moral and linguistic maturation proceed on very set lines. Children make particular grammatical errors at particular stages in their development and their ethics mature likewise stage-wise. And a fourth similarity is that moral and linguistic competence are both affected by specific learning difficulties and brain abnormalities.

These are striking similarities. Yet from the surety of linguistic intuitions no one has ever attempted to argue for God: 'The certainty of my grammatical judgments and the mysteriousness of their origin are together so marvellous that they can only be explained by invoking God'.[16] Certainty of moral intuitions makes no more convincing a case. In fact, the contrary is true. All the linguistic facts mentioned reveal that human linguistic competence has a very systematic nature, making it susceptible to scientific study. For which reason, linguistics now exists as a science: the search for a Universal Grammar, the template of human languages. This raises the possibility that moral intuitions might form the subject of a similar science of the psyche: Universal Goodness, the template of human ethics. It would hardly be surprising should such a thing exist. Humans are social animals. Our society, like that of any social animals, depends, in part, on our acceptance of certain standards. One cannot build the tower of Babel if everyone uses different words and different grammar. Nor can one if everyone has different morals, permitting some to steal building materials, others not to work, others to kill the slackers, and so on. The possibility of an explanation of our moral intuitions' origin and nature undermines the argument from ethics to God.

I said that the Argument from Ethics raises two questions. The matter of (in)correctness has now been dealt with. Now I want to discuss the impact of the incorrect association of moral intuitions with God. This at last will fulfil the promise to frame the discussion of various historical facts concerning religion and ethical behaviour.

We have accepted that atheist and theist alike have moral intuitions. In addition, the theist believes that moral intuitions reveal God's will, which we must follow. For the theist, there is nothing worthier, nothing holier than doing God's bidding. Suppose that an atheist and a theist, intent on doing good, see that a course of action will have great benefits to a large number of people. Provision of prophylactics to sub-Saharan women, for example. For the well-intentioned atheist, there is every reason to follow the course of action. However, things are different for the theist, because of the desire to conform to God's will. If God's will conflicts with a way to do good, then conformity to God's will takes precedence over doing good. Which means that it is easier for the atheist to do good than for the theist.

The converse applies too. Suppose that an atheist and a theist, intent on avoiding evil, see that a course of action will create misery for many. Denying women proper access to medical assistance. For the atheist, there is every reason to avoid the course of action. But if the theist believes God wills the course of action, then misery is mandatory. Which means that it is easier for the atheist to avoid evil than for the theist.

Whether God's bidding results in happiness or in misery is an issue independent of questions of morality. This destructive doctrine becomes even more harmful when combined with a belief in Divine Inscrutability. God being superior to us in all aspects, we would be impudent to question His purpose. This is the perfect salve for conscience and compunctions. In fact, if one's actions are necessary for God's purpose and if one cannot see how, all the better, for one's befuddlement underscores God's superior understanding of Things In The Long Run and high-lights the futility of questioning His purpose. This century, with its waves of genocide, has shown us that individuals will stoop lowest when higher powers are responsible for the outcome of their actions.

Now, I am not for a moment suggesting that fanaticism or cruelty follow wherever moral codes are coupled with God. It would be absurd to claim that birth control, morality and theism are incompatible. I am merely pointing out that the association of God with morality is a dangerous one. There is a very natural chain of reasoning, an open and inviting path, from ethics founded in God to a God foundering in cruelty and immorality. Weakness of the human constitution makes that path a tempting excursion, a path much travelled by. It is the task of the next section to show how popular that path has been and to what perversion of morality belief in God has led.

The lasting impact of these thoughts is one of irony: irony that the opening question of this section achieves the opposite of its aim. According to the theists' picture, it is very easy for the atheist to be moral. God's moral code is in all people. So, since they are people, atheists need only introspect to find the path to goodness. However, theists must juggle their innate goodness with their acquired belief in God's will. They believe that to be moral is God's bidding and that God's bidding determines morality. But, if they make a mistake about what God wills, then they err. Such errors do occur. But only theists, who attempt to attune to God's will, are able or liable to make them. That is, misjudgment of God's will is a source of error, so belief in God's will is a course to error. That course affects the theist alone. This, then, turns the argument from ethics on its head. The question is not *How can you be moral without God?* It is *How can you be moral with Him?*

Religion and (im)morality

We are discussing morality and God. Until now, the point has been philosophical. We have been exploring the connections between God and good: whether one entails or requires the other. The answer was no. Moreover, God is far from being the foundation of morality. The relevant concepts and consequences make one expect morality and theism to be quite distinct, even distant. This section shows that the expectation is true. Many points are pertinent. I shall limit myself in this section to a few as they pertain to Christianity, the religion most relevant to our society. In the following section, I consider whether religion in general and Christianity in particular can be exculpated of vice in virtue of some notion of true religion or true Christianity. The catalogue of religion's wrong is balanced by discussion of atheism's shortcomings in the section after that, and then, in the final part of this chapter, I consider briefly what could constitute an atheist ethic.

Leafing through the history of religion is like scanning a catalogue of human evil. God's shadowy presence lurking in the wings, man has heaped more misery on his neighbour than any decent person would care to imagine. Christianity, far from taking the moral high ground, has revelled in the muck, consigning the innocent to rack, stake, gallows, and any other instrument of torture that its auspices could contrive. The virtuosic breadth in invention and infliction of misery that Christianity and Christians have displayed in the service of their God cannot fail to astound even the most cynical observer. Whether at the local level or across continents and oceans, that creative flair for destructive behaviour burns like a beacon, a monument to the worst excesses of human evil.

At its height, Christian institutions controlled or influenced every sphere of life, from the daily run of small communities to the shape of foreign policies of major powers. In all, it was often a source of ill. Twisted liturgies poured from the pulpits of Europe drawing litanies of horrors in their wake. Examples abound. James Vitry, who died in 1240, was Cardinal Bishop of Tusculum. In his sermons, he would include stories to entertain and educate his audience. One of the themes he thought worthy of attention was woman.

I heard of a man who had a tree in his garden in which two of his wives hanged themselves. One of his neighbours said to him, 'That tree is very lucky to be sure and has a good omen. I too have a bad wife. I ask you to give me a shoot from it to plant in my garden.'

In another excursus on women and matrimony, he recalled:

I once passed through a town in France where a ham or side of bacon had been hung in the street. It would be given to whomever could swear that his marriage had been contracted in such a way that he had been able to live with his wife for a whole year without regretting it. And, though it hung there for ten years, not a man had been found who could win the side of bacon, because within a year of the marriage's being contracted, it was regretted.

This misogynous message, coming from such an authority, must have taught many men contempt for matrimony and must have caused the denigration and suffering of as many women.

Unfortunately, there is nothing unusual in this attitude. Misogyny was rife in Christianity. Woman after all had seduced man away from God, which marked her as needing both strict control and harsh punishment. Even God, in his design of woman, colluded in her punishment, making labour and birth painful and perilous. In trials for witchcraft, black-artistry, and other satanic practices, women were more often accused than men and the 'trials' tortured and tormented the accused into distraction before condemning them to a gruesome death. And all this was justified in God's name, by people who believed that they were doing His bidding.

Such deplorable attitudes continue today. We are all used to the tendency of the ignorant to 'explain' the inexplicable, extraordinary and awful by invoking God. Epidemics, for instance, are often seen as God's handiwork, retribution for our evil. Several decades ago, syphilis wreaked havoc across the world. Transmitted by sexual intercourse, resulting in deafness, dementia and death, it was seen by many religious as God's punishment against the lascivious. Only a nature crippled by dogma could regard with satisfaction suffering and deaths of thousands. Innocent, monogamous or monoandrous spouses suffered for their partners' infidelity, and innocent infants were born to abnormally short and painful lives. Yet such suffering has not been enough to silence such moralists. When AIDS began to creep through the homosexual community, religionists once again detected Divine retribution. The protracted and painful deaths brought by AIDS were what those who had shunned God and nature deserved. A clergyman, asked what we should make of the tragedy of AIDS, suggested that perhaps we should simply not view it as a tragedy. Once again, as the extent of the AIDS epidemic in Africa, South East Asia, and elsewhere becomes apparent, such voices have become quieter. But have they learned the lesson or will they continue to watch with satisfaction, perceiving the hand of God in the suffering of others?

The wrong religions wrought within communities had its parallels without. The treatment of Europe's Jewry can only be described as sadistic. These culminated in recent times in the silence with which the Vatican greeted the Holocaust. Despite ample information and exhortation to act, Pope Pius XII observed the exportation and extermination of Italy's Jews in pure passivity. Recently, the Vatican has attempted to exculpate itself by claiming the anti-Semitism of the Holocaust to be distinct from the anti-Judaism typifying much of Catholicism's past – as if feeding maggots were not part of breeding flies. An acquaintance with few facts is enough to undermine the distinction. On the one hand, there were the events in local communities, such the Easter sermons that preceded riots and murders, the kidnappings and forced conversions. On the other, there was the behaviour of the highest Catholic authorities. In Venice, the Jewish ghetto flooded annually and yet, after each flood, its residents were forced to appear before Church authorities to beg for the right to remain where they were. In Rome, new popes on the way to the Vatican pass by the leaders of the Jewish community to deliver a ritual insult. In addition to restrictions on where they might live, Jews were forbidden from owning land

and from holding various jobs. When similar restrictions were imposed on the blacks of South Africa, the government was labelled racist and rightly so. It at least did not to try to defend itself by invoking a distinction between 'anti-black-ism' and 'anti-blackness-ism'.

No major brand of Christianity fares well in its relationship to Jews. The Orthodox Slavic Christianity, though separated from the Catholics by the schism, shared with them an intense anti-Semitism. The Chmieicki uprising of 1648, the pogroms of the nineteenth century, and the later persecution of Soviet Jewry, all were founded on the anti-Semitism preached in Slavic pulpits. The Protestant revolution looked more promising for Jews. The spread of vernacular copies of the Old Testament brought a new understanding of Jews and Martin Luther preached tolerance. Unfortunately, Luther's tolerance was not a humanitarian principle. It was based on the belief that Jews had not converted because of Catholics' cruelty towards them. He did much to build bridges between Jews and Christians. In 1523, he wrote a pamphlet entitled 'That Jesus Christ was a Jew by Birth'. He was even portrayed holding a Hebrew book (upside-down). His soft approach too failed, however. 'Of Jews and Their Lies' appeared in 1542, urging that the synagogues, schools, and houses of 'that perverse, damned people' be burned, that rabbis be threatened with death if found teaching Talmud or prayer. His fury at those who rejected his teaching is reminiscent of Jesus'.

When Europe learned of the Americas and Australia, the shadow of Christianity stretched across the ocean, wreaking havoc and wrecking lives. In South America, conquistadors would baptise abducted infants then dash their brains out on rocks, sending their freshly saved souls straight to heaven, preserving them from a heathen life of sin.[17] In North America, the same mixture of mission and massacre was mounted. Called 'the land of freedom', its early settlers envisaged in particular religious freedom. Many of the pioneer pilgrims had fled religious persecution – another consequence of the confusion of moral conduct with conformity to religious precepts. Sectarian wars were common. This, together with the attempts of missionaries to convert his followers, prompted the Seneca chief Sagoyewatha to wonder about Christianity.

> Brother, you say there is but one way to worship and serve the Great Spirit. If there is but one religion, why do you white people differ so much about it? Why are not all agreed, if you can all read the Book?[18]

His reaction to the attempted conversion of his followers was to wait and see.

> We will wait a little while and see what effect your preaching has on them [our white neighbours]. If we find it does make them good, makes them honest, and less disposed to cheat Indians, we will then consider again of what you have said.

That is, in the pursuit of morality and religion, he employed somewhat Spartan and meritocratic ideals.

All the events mentioned above have two elements in common. Firstly, they were cruel and despicable. Secondly, they were sanctioned or incited by religion, by the belief that the deeds were what God wanted. All illustrate that religion and belief in God, far from being the foundation of moral behaviour, are often an impediment to it.

The theist at this point will do one of two things: object or convert. One objection is that, in all of the above incidents, Christianity and Christ's teachings were abused. There is a real Christianity, a correct interpretation of Christ's word. The horrors mentioned resulted from misinterpretation. Alternatively, the non-Christian might say that the problems mentioned belong to Christianity specifically, and not to other theistic systems. In either case, I could be accused of having ignored the good that religion has inspired. A different tack is to claim that atheism's crimes are every bit as bad as theism's. The Nazi and Soviet regimes are cases in point. So, atheism cannot claim the upper hand. Let's consider each objection, for, though misguided, we stumble on some interesting realisations when reorienting ourselves to the truth.

True Christianity?

Before addressing whether the historical events outlined above illustrate 'fake Christianity', as presumably the opposite of true Christianity is called, I want to mention briefly other religions. Happy to see Christianity in the hot seat, other religionists might claim that the problems unearthed are problems with Christianity and not with theism in general.

This is not the place to enter into a detailed almanac of religious wrongdoing. However, it requires little effort on the part of the reader to track down such events. For the moment, it suffices to say that no religion can claim purity. The internal politics of Iran and Afghanistan say all that is necessary for Islam. The behaviour of the religious right wing in Israel likewise smears Judaism. Hinduism, too, has fundamentalist threads. Even Buddhism, the darling of modern Western spiritualists, has had its share of religious wars. The religion, for instance, came with wars into Tibet, the opposing sides led by brothers. The general point pursued with respect to Christianity, that religion spawns ill, can be translated to other religions, provided they have had power and time enough to incriminate themselves.

Returning to Christianity, the question is whether the religion has a Jekyll-and-Hyde existence, whether there is a Christianity, called 'true', which is entirely benign and desirable, and which must be distinguished from the malignant alter ego responsible for the atrocities described above. Adherents of true Christianity would be Mother Teresa, who battled against illness and poverty, and William Wilberforce, who fought against slavery. Such people understood and embodied the goodness and humanity that represents the message of the 'real' Jesus.

We must ask two questions of this attempt to rehabilitate the respectability of Christianity: whether it is accurate and whether it is relevant. Does it hit the nail on the head and does it hit the right nail? The answer to both is negative. Accuracy is discussed below. As for relevance, there is the matter of whether there is any point in attempting to discover true Christianity. The fact would remain that for thousands of years Christian text and Christian teaching have inspired evil in some and good in others. Attempts to unearth the real meaning of Christ's word are compatible with the incompatible behaviour of saints and savages. Given the wide range of incompatible interpretations to be drawn from Jesus' teaching, the only conclusion is that what-ever he had to say is simply and radically ill-suited to the foundation of a stable society. Moreover, when clerics attempt to influence government policy, making it resemble God's will or law, we should recognise how deeply suspect such advice must be. This theme is the topic of Chapter 6.

Consider the claim that there is a true Christianity based on what Christ really said. For that claim to mean anything, we must be able to know what true Christianity is. It is not sufficient to say that true Christians are moral people. For then we are deciding first what morality is and then deciding who are the true Christians. No wonder then that all true Christians are moral. No wonder that Christ's real bidding leads to goodness. However, that is clearly a fudge. If the claim is to mean anything, then we must be able to know what the precepts of true Christianity are. By definition, we are discounting history of Christianity as the source of that knowledge. So, either we look to the New Testament itself, or we trust others who claim to know the truth by being holy themselves. The last option is not an option. For, suppose our guru were Jo Smith. How would we tell the difference between true Christianity interpreted by J. Smith and a new faith called Smithtianity? The only alternative for true Christianity is a close reading of the New Testament.

So, the question is whether Christ was a holy man whose every dictum and edict we could follow without fear of trespass. The first problem we encounter is that the Gospels, which purport to report the life and works of Jesus, were written well after the events they relate. Their authorship is doubtful. Some are believed to be the work of several authors. Their purpose was not to tell the truth. They were propaganda in a political and sectarian battle. They plagiarised, or quoted, Old Testament texts in a bid to create from Jesus a messiah. They vilified their opponents and in that vilification they laid a groundwork of animosity and antipathy that would distil over centuries into a potent anti-Semitism. However, if we are clever enough to know that the documents are hashed and rehashed, then perhaps we are clever enough to detect the real Jesus beneath the propaganda.

Undeniably, there is much to be admired in Jesus' aphorisms and actions. Jesus advocated pacifism: 'Resist not evil, but whosoever shall smite thee on thy right cheek, turn to him the other also'. This noble admonition runs through many disparate schools of thought, many older than Christianity. Eastern thinkers such Gautama Buddha professed it. Mahatma Gandhi and the Dalai Lama have earned respect and admiration by practising it. Of course, as a prelude to being the victim of genocide, the maxim should not be taken too far. However, its emphasis on the nobility of the human spirit in adversity should be a source of inspiration. Jesus' commendation of being generous and non-judgmental would also, if followed, surely have a positive influence on the world. 'Judge not lest ye be judged.' 'Give to him that asketh thee and from him that would borrow of thee turn not thou away.'

Curiously, Christians rarely seem troubled to heed their God's word. They are forever judging others. Their glasshouses are full of stones. They are all too willing to ignore the needy. Certainly, one encounters almost none who have followed Christ's teaching on giving and lending to the fullest extent: 'If thou wilt be perfect, go and sell that thou hast, and give to the poor'. In fact, a truly Christian society would have to be one where no one were ever punished, where no one owned or owed anything, and which would give any portion of its wealth to any individual or organisation that asked for it. Is such a state desirable?

Some of Christ's teachings, then, are admirable when dilute, even if caustic to the human weft when neat. Yet the New

Testament reveals Jesus as decidedly flawed. When ignored, Jesus became petulant. He labelled his detractors 'serpents', a 'generation of vipers'. When mocked, he became vindictive. He envisaged for his enemies an eternity of 'wailing and gnashing of teeth' in 'a furnace of fire', 'everlasting fire', 'fire [that] is not quenched', 'where the worm dieth not'. The doctrine of everlasting torture has justified such inhumanity and caused terror in children, adults, the elderly and the dying that it cannot be the work of a humane person.

Anthony Storr has examined many different cult figures, trying to define what defines a guru. In *Feet of Clay*, he examines all sorts of iconoclastic, iconified men: Jung and Freud, Gurdjieff and Rajneesh, and Jesus. What he reveals is that Jesus' petulance and vindictiveness are entirely typical, though not universal. Gurus are 'teachers who claim special knowledge of the meaning of life, and who therefore feel entitled to tell others how life should be lived'.[19] They believe themselves to know the truth, usually by personal revelation, and their followers believe them to too. They are often dismissive of detractors, derisive and damning. Jesus' attitude is not surprising, therefore. It reveals him merely to be one amongst many cast in the same psychological mould. Moreover, Geza Vermes' study of Jesus the Jew reveals him to be one of potentially many cast in the same cultural mould. In that light, he does not shine as particularly holy, nor do his teachings seem, except in some instances, commendable. They are not the key to saving either society or self.

Immoral atheism

I am trying to reach a conclusion in this circuitous discussion of morality and theism. And the conclusion I am aiming for is that, if we wish the world to be a just and peaceful place, inhabited by just and peaceable people, then we will reach our goal far faster if we are atheists than if we are theists. This will then be another argument that atheism is superior to theism, additional to the purely theoretical argument over worldviews that began this book. Ironically, the argument will be drawn from an attempt to undermine the opening argument by claiming moral behaviour to be inextricable from God. Before I can claim that, however, there is one more hurdle.

'The deliberate lie in religion' was, said Hitler in July 1941, its claim 'to bring men to liberty, only to enslave them'.[20] The Marxist regime to which Stalin nominally aspired was by definition 'godless' and he had ridiculed religion since attending a seminary in his adolescence. Both Hitler's Germany and Stalin's Russia were intended as atheist regimes. Yet we are all familiar with the excesses of their inhumanity. Having already concluded that the cruelty to which theism leads is evidence against the idea that morality must be tied to God, are we now forced, by parity of reasoning, to say that atheism, leading to equal inhumanity, is equally ill-suited to underpinning morality? Theists often claim something like that. When religion is attacked for leading to suffering, they point to the regimes of Hitler, Stalin and others to show that atheism is equally evilly adept. The Archbishop of Canterbury, who is open-minded and even-handed in these matters, has said, for instance: 'those who dwell on the alleged destructive power of religions in world affairs ..., might want to reflect on the mass slaughter of civilians in concentration camps and elsewhere, carried out by the messianic but secular regimes presided over by Stalin and Hitler and Pol Pot. These it can be argued are examples where the absence of true religion, and the abandonment of basic moral values anchored in it, helped to make genocide both possible and, shamefully, acceptable.'[21]

No one will deny the evil of Hitler and Stalin (though, given the preceding section, the allusion to 'true religion' should now be clearly spurious). However, is that enough for the theist to win the argument? Specifically, is their evil atheism's evil, and how would that affect the general line pursued here, that we are better off with the Spartan meritocracy, which leads to atheism, than with the Baroque monarchy, of which theism is an instance?

As before, both these arguments backfire on the theist. Despite the nominal atheism of their regimes, Hitler and Stalin owed much to religion. Moreover, their regimes, though atheist, were both Baroque monarchies.

It is generally known of Stalin that he had a religious education. From 1894 until 1899, when he was nearly twenty, Stalin attended the Russian Orthodox seminary at Tiflis, now Tblisi. Alan Bullock wrote of his education:

> The fact that it was a Church education helped to form the mind of a man who was to become known for his dogmatism and his propensity for seeing issues in absolute terms, in black and white. Anyone reading Stalin's speeches and writings will notice their catechistic structure, the use of question and answer, the reduction of complex questions to a set of simplified formulas, the quoting of texts to support his arguments. The same Church influence has been noted by biographers in his style of speaking or writing Russian: 'declamatory and repetitive, with liturgical overtones'.[22]

The Church had its influence on Hitler too, in the shape of Catholicism rather than Slavic Orthodoxy. Raised Catholic, Hitler had developed a strong admiration for the Church. Rome had 'a religion you can take seriously', 'a great position to defend'[23], one that had endured for centuries. Though he could hardly have been more dismissive of its teaching, he admired its organisation and power. He claimed to have learned much from its skilful manipulation of human nature.

The effect of religion on the leaders of these regimes is not the only relevant point. There is also its effect on the led. One must wonder how much success Stalin's method and manner would have had if his audience had not already been accustomed to sermonising. Similarly, if the Church had not for so long terrorised its followers with tales of the devil in disguise, of infiltration and subjugation by Satan, Stalin might not have found such powerful weapons in fictional external threats and enemies within. Hitler's myths of Aryan congenital superiority and Slavic congenital inferiority must have owed much to the idea propounded by the Church that man is born evil though he had enjoyed an ancient purity. His treatment of Jews, their being banned from specific jobs, their being forced to wear distinctive clothing, their being forced to walk in the gutter, and much else, all stem from Mediaeval Christianity.

We are concerned with the claim that theism cannot be justly criticised as a source of evil because Nazism and Stalinism were atheist systems and they were just as evil as theistic ones. I have argued that the particular examples of Nazism and Stalinism are bad choices because theism, Christianity in particular, must bear much of the responsibility for their evil. The Kingdom of Heaven, the New Testament of Matthew informs us, is like a man who readies his field for sowing only to have his neighbour steal in at night to sow it with corn-cockle. Yet, the first man tends both and reaps both. Centuries of Church dogma furrowed the fields ready for Hitler and Stalin's seeds. Certainly, the Catholic and Russian Orthodox Churches tended the crop, actively or silently, to varying degrees at varying times. By the corn-cockle gospel, they must reap the consequences.

Faced with the failure of Hitler and Stalin as examples, the theist might be tempted to look to other nominally atheist tyrants, to Africa or to Asia. However, there is no point. Or rather, there is a point and looking elsewhere misses it. For there is something that Christianity, other religions, Nazism, Stalinism, Communism, and other tyrannical isms all share: they are to varying degrees dogmatic. All present their adherents with a set of doctrines that they must accept. In the case of Nazism, they were doctrines of racial inferiority and superiority in a framework of spurious pseudoscience. In the case of Stalinism, they were Marxist ideals of social reform and progress based on a pseudoscientific reading of history. In either case, failure to conform to the dogma led to a fate similar to that which followed failure to conform to religious dogma: a combination of public humiliation, show trials, punishment, being ostracised, exile, and death. The dogma justified persecution within the society and persecution by the society.

The issue then is not whether atheism in any shape is better than theism. The issue is the effect of dogma on human goodness. And that effect is negative. In other words, I concede the theist's point. It *is* unfair to castigate religion alone as a systematic source of evil. The source of evil is dogma, the belief that there is a set of principles that is entirely right and can justify, exculpate and motivate any act in their service. When a society values the failure to question its guiding principles, when utter obedience is admirable, then what the society truly values is not the principles, but authority and conformity. In such cases, whether or not God is part of the system, it is only a matter of time before someone arises to manipulate the authority or before the group uses its conformity as the yardstick by which to condemn others, inside or outside, who do not conform.

The source of evil then is the Baroque monarchy. The belief that a set of principles can be preordained as right, proper, or correct, without regard to their effect in practice, and the belief that such principles are absolute truths, unquestionable and unrevisable – these have emerged as the target of the criticism above. These beliefs are Baroque and monarchic respectively. Nazism and Stalinism are Baroque monarchies without God. Religions are Baroque monarchies with Him. The greatest impediment to goodness, it seems, is dogma, which warps the human spirit, killing off its compassion and goodness, replacing it with blind obedience. Yet we need compassion and goodness and should shun blind obedience. This entails shunning dogma, which in turn entails shunning the Baroque monarchy as a worldview. And that entails shunning theism.

Atheist ethics

We now have a second argument for the superiority of atheism over theism. In certain respects, it is the opposite of the first argument, which was founded on abstract considerations about what makes a plausible worldview. The second argument is concerned with something far more practical: the ethics that underpin our daily behaviour. The conclusion reached is that dogma, central to the Baroque monarchy, is the greatest impediment to morality. So, if you are concerned to be moral, you are better off without theism, which is such a monarchy.

But what are the ethics of the Spartan meritocracy? That worldview is a methodology of questions and justification. Its methods are not merely suited to issues of science and nature. Centuries of rational philosophy have shown them to be well suited to moral enquiry. Mill's Utilitarianism, Hobbes' Leviathan, Rawls' theory of social justice are all examples of Spartan assumptions subjected to rigorous tests of merit with a view to shaping via reason a moral individual in an ethical society.

In fact, as our society increases in complexity, both internally, in the variety of rights and rightholders that it recognises, and externally, in its relationship with others, we come to rely ever more on moral concepts and mechanisms that are inherently atheist, Spartan, and meritocratic. To take but one example, consider voting and voting reform. The aim of voting is to ensure that government be representative. But how can one be representative of a heterogeneous society with mutually incompatible beliefs? What constitutes a fair voting process for such a society? Precisely these questions, and related ones, are the subject matter of mathematical decision theory, a rational discipline, both Spartan and meritocratic. Despite its forbidding, abstract name, its results are of the deepest practical significance to democracies or any system that aims to be fair, just, and representative. An indicator of this significance may be that two of the greatest decision theorists, Kenneth Arrow and Amartya Sen, are Nobel laureates.

Just as the Spartan meritocracy provides the investigation of nature, not with answers, but with a framework in which to seek answers, so it is with the investigation of ethics. Of course, this does not offer the immediate gratification of religious doctrine, but perhaps it is good for one not always to be immediately gratified.

What we abhor in theistic 'ethics' is the cruelty to others and the debasement of the individual that they entail. These arise because of overriding subservience to a dogma. In a meritocratic system, if a proposed moral principle were seen to lead to cruelty, it would be rejected because the principle is always secondary to the aim of moral action. This contrasts to a Baroque monarchy, where everything is secondary to the starting assumptions. The Spartan meritocrat, then, has to ask, at each stage, whether his or her actions lead to good. If the answer is negative, then (s)he must behave differently. That is the principle at any rate. I cannot pretend that it is always easy to answer the question: *'Will my actions have a positive impact or will they lead to cruelty, misery ...?'* For one thing, notions such as positive and negative are notoriously difficult to pin down. Recall in the discussion of the tram and the surgeon how difficult it was to pinpoint the criterion distinguishing moral from immoral actions. The search for adequate answers is arduous. However, altruism, compassion, and goodness in other guises come naturally to us. Their cultivation must be an imperative of any moral code. Dogma, however, is a parasite that cripples or destroys sapling morality. Even if all other answers to questions of morality are obscure, we know this much: a well-considered atheism is a much surer path to it than dogma-ridden theism.

Conclusion

I have been examining the commonly held view that theism, God, or religion are fundamental to morality. Similar arguments exist that they are fundamental to other elements of the good life. The point of considering such arguments was to decide whether they mollify, or undermine, the conclusion of the first chapter, that the Spartan meritocracy and atheism are superior to the Baroque monarchy and theism. The idea was that we want to be happy, moral, well-rounded beings and that this requires religion or some form of the Baroque monarchy, as the good life is a topic often appropriated by religion and ignored by rational enquiry.

My response has facets. On the one hand, I observed that there is a very large body of investigation into goodness, justice, fairness, morality, both de- and prescriptive, that is Spartan and meritocratic. This includes developmental and adult psychology, and analytic philosophy and theories of justice. Therefore, the Spartan meritocrat is not destined to a life of misery and immorality. On the other hand, I argued that there are philosophical reasons to expect theism to be an impediment to moral behaviour. A perusal of history shows the expectation correct. The source of the problem is dogma, the heart of the Baroque monarchy, or religion, and of theism.

All these facts present a second argument for atheism's superiority over theism. In addition to the superiority in theory outlined earlier in the book, we now have superiority in practice too.

Chapter 5

Individuals and Intuitions

Believe in His prophets – Chronicles II 20:20

In this chapter, I will consider three types of people whose existence might be considered to challenge the atheist position that
it has been the aim of the last four chapters to support. The first
are religious scientists. As I have been arguing religion and
science to be the fruits of opposite worldviews, scientific experts
who believe in God may seem to threaten the conclusions drawn
so far. On the other hand, there are spiritualists, psychics, and so
on, 'spiritual experts' whose specialness may be thought to
confer extra weight on their belief in God. The purpose of this
chapter is to consider these walking, talking arguments for God.
In the course of the discussion, I fulfil one of the aims of the
preceding chapter, mentioned also in Chapter 1. I detailed the
successes of applying Spartan, meritocratic ideals to the investigation of the world as well as to the pursuit of morality, etc. I also
detailed the failure of Baroque, monarchic ideals in the search for
morality, etc. The possibility of Baroque, monarchic ideals
applied to the investigation of Nature has not yet been considered. This occurs below.

Religious scientists

In the previous chapter, I considered whether we need a compromise between the two opposite worldviews that I have been
calling the Spartan meritocracy and the Baroque monarchy. Of
course, the two positions are in friction and it would be very

confusing if we were forced to adopt both. Yet, it appears that some people both understand them and accept them. They are religious scientists, who believe in the efficacy of the scientific method and yet believe in a deity. As scientists, they adhere, in practice, to the Spartan meritocracy. As believers, they adhere to some Baroque monarch. What are we to make of this accommodation? Does it undermine the position I have been arguing for, in which rational atheism and theism are not merely different answers to the question of God's existence but rather diametric opposites?

Religious scientists are inclined to take a wide variety of positions. On the one hand, there are the likes of Einstein, who believe in a personal deity, defined in a way that suits their personal tastes. On the other hand, there are the likes of Mohammed Abdus Salam, joint recipient of the 1979 Nobel Prize for physics, who adhere to an established religion – Islam in Salam's case. And there are other positions. In all cases, such men and women would disagree with my claim that theism and science belong to incompatible worldviews and that one must choose between them. Am I really going to say that such erudite people as Einstein were outright not right?

In brief, yes, I believe they were wrong. A certain reticence sets in when it comes to criticising Einstein. That is hardly surprising given his genius. However, like any scientist, he made errors. Essentially, he was an intuitionist: he had hunches and his hunches were good. But, at the crunch, some will be off. This is most famously the case with his 'no dicing deity' dictum, in which he expressed his doubt that quantum mechanics' reliance on probability could represent the universe truly. At the time, there was no firm evidence either way. In 1964, however, Bell found an area where quantum mechanics and relativity made different predictions, placed different limits, now known as the Bell inequalities, on the accuracy of measurements under particular circumstances. Sixteen years later, the circumstances were contrived and the measurements taken. In that key experiment, quantum mechanics was vindicated: *alea iacta erat*. The moral is that no one's intuition is infallible. If we recognise the fallibility of Einstein's intuitions in physics, the area in which we most respect his opinions, then we can surely entertain that his intuitions were wrong elsewhere, too.

For the Spartan meritocracy to be viable as a worldview, its methods should reveal truths about the universe and its implementation in the day-to-day should conduce to a fulfilling existence. Now, science is Spartan, meritocratic enquiry into nature. Nowhere are the mental states of the enquirer mentioned as significant to the outcome of the enquiry. In fact, the opposite is true. Because the success of the Spartan meritocracy is independent of the beliefs of its practitioners, we come to a simple expectation: the beliefs of the practitioner are irrelevant (so long as they do not interfere with the enquiry). That is just what we see: scientists' (dis)agreement in scientific matters is independent of their (dis)belief in God. In other words, the existence of religious scientists supports the conclusions reached so far, that the Spartan meritocracy is an outstandingly successful paradigm, one that cannot be ignored.

So, it presents no problem – indeed the contrary is true – for the Spartan meritocracy that people who use it to investigate nature do not apply it elsewhere. The same non-problem arises elsewhere, as when technology-users embrace the implementation of the science that arises by methods they otherwise reject. Just as it is possible to use a microwave oven without regard to the edifice of science that underlies the technology, so it is possible to apply the methods of rational enquiry within a limited domain, such as nuclear physics, without regard to the methods' wider implications. Those wider implications include philosophical issues concerning the nature of the world and the enquiry into it, issues that, I have argued, are closely tied to a commitment to atheism. But knowing the answers to these questions is neither necessary nor sufficient for being a great scientist, leaving room within the Spartan meritocracy for religious scientists.

Religious science

There is, however, another interpretation of the existence of theist scientists, which affords them much more significance than I have above. One might question whether religious scientists are doing the same science as atheist scientists. Consider for example, the Nobel Laureate Mohammed Abdus Salam, a devout Muslim. If science forms part of Salam's religious worldview, the discovery of God's machinery, say, then his science might be argued to be Islamic Science, as it stems from (conforms to, is allied with) Islamic belief. On such a view, science is the study of God's creation. Such a view of science is essentially an attempt to reconcile it with religion by making science part of theology, investigation of the world under some Baroque monarch's auspices. It is a project taken very seriously in some quarters, as manifested by the number of conferences, organisations and websites dedicated to the cause. In fairness to Salam, I must say outright that he does not subscribe to any version of Islamic Science.[24] His mention here is purely illustrative.

Islamic Science belongs to a host of 'alternative' sciences that have been given increasing attention as postmodernist concepts have gained acceptance. Sibling 'alternatives' are Marxist Science and Third World Science – Feminist Epistemology is of the same genus. Such 'alternatives' suppose that modern science is Western Science and that its conclusions can be no more universal than Western culture and values are universal. As culture and values vary throughout the world, so science ought to vary. If there were a successful Islamic Science or Marxist Science, there would indeed be a problem for the line followed here. So much of the support for the Spartan meritocracy comes from the enormous success of its implementation in the investigation of nature. If equal success could be achieved by implementing a different worldview, then that support for Sparta crumbles. So, let me explain what these alternative sciences are like and then ask whether they are successful enough to unsettle the conclusions reached so far.

Islamic Science, its social circumstances, its nature, and its practitioners are examined in Pervez Hoodbhoy's *Islam and Science*. However, before considering it, a couple of caveats deserve mention.

Christianity long ago learned the peril of attempting to make science part of theology. The idea is attractive so long as science is fledgling with little to say. Under such circumstances, religion's story of how the world works and how we have come to exist goes unchallenged. Science is appealing because it promises to catalogue God's wonders and to reveal the magnificence of His work. However, as science matures, it can discover facts that contradict God's version of events, as told in religious texts. When conflict arises, it may be religion that is forced to back down. This has broadly been the case in the West, where the success of science has forced the reluctant relinquishment of a literal reading of the Bible. It is now interpreted as metaphor, that is, it is accepted as literally false. From the revolution of planets to the evolution of humans, even the Catholic Church, that denizen of dogma, has recognised that the Bible, supposedly authored, or coauthored, by God himself, was written in fact by people who were largely ignorant of the mechanisms of creation. Now, of course, religion can withstand having its central texts rendered a metaphor. However, to set rational enquiry amongst theology's disciplines is to set the stage for mutiny within the ranks. That is the first caveat: that free reign to rational enquiry can damage the authority of dogma.

The second caveat concerns an attempt to avoid the problem identified in the first, namely, the attempt to reshape science along dogmatic lines. An example of this is Stalinist Science, an attempt to show that the insentient world adhered to or was compatible with the doctrines of the Stalinist Soviet Union. Stalin wished to rid his regime of all Western influences, including Western science, which was to be supplanted by a homegrown genius. Trofim Lysenko, one of Stalinist Science's chief practitioners, advocated 'Michurinism', the doctrine that Nature was changeable and that acquired characteristics were inheritable. Now, Slavic scientists had been instrumental in launching the study of genes and inheritance. However, the leaders, such as Gregor Mendel, were, naturally, members of the social elite and enemies of Soviet principles. (In Mendel's famous experiment of the pea-plants, the plants were tended by monks.) Michurin earned favour by being of peasant stock, by being self-educated, and by expounding a philosophy that proved man capable of overcoming putative 'natural laws'. Michurinism was proletarian science. When Lysenko's Michurinist proposals were criticised by the scientific establishment, he returned the assault, but on ideological, not scientific, grounds. His detractors, practitioners of bourgeois genetics, were reactionaries, opposed to his application of Marxist principles to genetics and to the broader socialist attempt to alter the environment. With Stalin's backing, Lysenko was sure to win and in 1948, following a conference at the Lenin Academy, Michurinism became the orthodoxy of Soviet science. Three thousand biologists lost their posts.

As a scientific theory, Michurinism has little except cautionary value to offer modern researchers. As the underpinning of technological innovation, it was a disaster. Soviet research into genetics was part of a wider push to advance methods of food production following the famine of 1946. In 1953, after death of Stalin and the myth that he had revived Soviet agriculture, Khrushchev revealed to the Supreme Soviet that in all areas of livestock production and agriculture[25], the country was still less productive than it had been at the start of the Second World War. Such was the success of Stalinist Science. The moral here is that when dogma limits the domain of enquiry, there is little chance for an increase in knowledge, whether theoretical or practical.

Islamic Science is well on its way to avoiding the problems highlighted by the first caveat. However, in heeding the first caveat, it falls foul of the second. Hoodbhoy cites the following samples of Islamic Science research. An earth sciences professor at Egypt's Al Ahzar university argues that mountains are tent pegs that stop things flying away as the earth rotates. An engineer, who worked in the Egyptian army in 1976, argues that God will destroy the world with copper shells empty of explosives, as these allow a 'better' build up of the destructive shock waves. A senior scientist at the Pakistan Council for Scientific and Industrial Research has discovered a mathematical formula for measuring how hypocritical a society is. And a senior member of the Pakistan Atomic Energy Commission at one point suggested obtaining energy by tapping jinns, a kind of fire creature – though he denied it in the *Wall Street Journal* eight years later. All these examples lack the hallmarks of good science: there are no hitherto unexplained phenomena that they unite and they tell us next to nothing about how the world will behave in situations that we have yet to observe. Nor do they have any practical applications in the real world, a sign that they have no finger on Nature's pulse.

But is the failure of Islamic Science inevitable? That is, is it possible to build such a new 'science' whilst heeding both caveats? The answer appears to be no. Science's success comes from its freedom of enquiry. No question is out of bounds, no answer is in principle unthinkable. To consider any question unaskable or any answer unconscionable would go against the Spartan meritocratic spirit, according to which all beliefs must be fully questioned if they are to be part of our worldview. To construct a 'science' that is founded on unquestionable dogma is to deprive enquiry of what it must have in order to be successful: freedom of thought. Because of the desire to restrict freedom of thought and enquiry, Islamic Science, just like Stalinist Science, must be doomed. If this is the correct conclusion, then there are no alternative sciences and so the existence of religious scientists cannot be explained by invoking Religious Science.

Reconciliation & the nature of the conflict

The recent discussion has focused on scientists whose theism suggests that the Spartan meritocracy and the Baroque monarchy are not so irreconcilable as I have made them seem. I considered two interpretations of their existence. They can be seen as showing science and religion to be compatible. Or they can be seen as showing that there must be a different form of science, a religious science, which is compatible with the Baroque monarchy but is as successful as the Spartan meritocracy. Both these interpretations are, I argued, incorrect. The nature of the errors is important however, because it reveals the fundamental flaw underlying much debate concerning atheism and theism. Both attempts to pin the respectability of theism on the respectability of particular theists, such as Einstein and Salam, portray the fundamental conflict as being between science and religion. I have said above why this is a mistake and I repeat it clearly now.

Science and religion are merely pieces in a larger puzzle. They are not the puzzle themselves. Science is the product of one paradigm, the Spartan meritocracy, a worldview that compels us to make as few binding assumptions about the nature of the world as is possible and to question what assumptions we do make. Another product of that paradigm is atheism – atheism follows given how the paradigm works and the way the world is. Religion, on the other hand, is the product of another paradigm, the Baroque monarchy, a worldview that designates a certain set of beliefs as privileged and unassailable. So, there are two apparent conflicts: atheism versus theism and science versus religion. The central claim of this book is that both these debates are secondary. The primary debate concerns the paradigms that underlie atheism and science on the one hand, and theism and religion on the other.

Given the conflict between the paradigms, it is hardly surprising to find conflict amongst the offspring. Yet it is not inevitable that there will be conflict amongst the offspring. There is agreement between religious ethics and the ethics of analytic philosophers, for instance. The existence of Einsteins and Salams is all but irrelevant to the (a)theist debate. At best it shows that there is no conflict between two offspring, loosely enough understood, of different paradigms. But it does not address the fundamental issue, namely, which of the two opposing paradigms we should adopt.

In this context, it is important to mention Stephen Gould's recent attempt 'to present a blessedly simple ... resolution to ...

the supposed conflict between science and religion', a resolution that 'follows a strong consensus accepted for decades by leading scientific and religious thinkers alike'.[26] Once, Gould says, religious explanation encompassed all; the nearest there was to an alternative explanation was an alternative religion and most knew nothing of those. Therefore, the 'magesterium of religion', or the domain of facts that it fell to religion to explain, was everything. Later, science arose and attempted to explain parts of religion's magisterium differently. This led to conflict, territorial in essence. Gould's solution is to recognise, as is perfectly obvious, that not every question is a scientific question. That is, if religion relinquishes part of what used to be its magisterium, then there will never again be conflict between science and religion because there will never be any fact for which they offer competing explanations.

The very goodness of Gould's proposal, and the happy coexistence to which it could lead, make me wish it were workable. But, unfortunately, I feel it misses the fundamental issues, as outlined above. It is not enough to observe, correctly, that not every question falls to science, in order to assure a happy domain for religion. The question is where the limits lie of the two world-views of which science and religion are part. And the whole point about Spartan, meritocratic enquiry is that it permits no borders to be drawn until all investigation is over. Belief, in the absence of argument, that there will be such a border is un-Spartan. Instituting such an unshifting border is unmeritocratic. And it is hard to see how Gould's truce will be maintained as we begin better to understand the human mind, both in terms of neurobiology and of psychological evolution – as science begins, that is, to consider the evolutionary basis of dogmatic conviction and the neurobiology of what we now nebulously name 'religious belief'.

Spiritual experts

In the preceding sections, I have considered the significance of a certain set of individuals for the tenability of theism, namely, religious scientists. Another set of individuals also sways many people's opinions in the (a)theism debate. They are what I shall call *spiritual experts*, people who claim special holiness, as do yogis, rabbis, lamas, tele-evangelists, or their followers, and others such as psychics and faith-healers. Many regard spiritual experts as flesh-and-blood arguments for God's existence. In brief, they reason that they are people with amazing abilities who believe in and attribute their abilities to God. Being special, such people's opinions are privileged. Their special abilities confer a certainty on their beliefs. They are spiritual experts to whom we must defer in regard to the existence of God and other mystical entities.

There are two types of spiritual experts to consider, the overtly spiritual and the covertly spiritual. By covertly spiritual, I mean people whose most distinguishing characteristic is an ability, such as the capacity to heal by touch. By overtly spiritual, I mean people who claim special access to God and His desires. As there is an abundance of both sorts, I shall take an example of each for concreteness, but the point of the discussion will always be to determine whether such people *in general* are proof of God's existence.

Personal intuitions

Before turning to the argument from attestations by spiritual experts, we should note a DIY version of the argument. The point of bringing spiritual experts into consideration is that their personal impressions are meant to carry weight. The DIY version of the argument misses out on the expert relying instead on the personal conviction of any theist who claims him- or herself able to intuit God's existence. Now, in my experience, such people are quite common. They claim to know that God exists because they have 'felt it'. Such personal encounters are given very high regard in some religious quarters, early Protestantism being one example, modern evangelism being another. Even the more staid Catholic Church holds as a matter of dogma that God's existence may be proved by means other than logic, which, by process of elimination, I can only think means some kind of experience. What then is to be made of such personal protestations?

Very little should be made of such personal protestations. People are constantly subject to the most extreme personal convictions, which they can in no way rationalise. However, strength of conviction never guarantees truth. When one person experiences the deepest personal conviction of one notion, say, that Jesus is the way, another person can experience with conviction just as deep an entirely incompatible notion, say, that Allah is the way. A more reasonable light in which to regard such occurrences is to suppose that there are some people who are disposed to experience extreme conviction and that the substance of the conviction, Jesus, Allah, or other, is entirely incidental.

The unreliability of such protestations can be made clearer by analogy to dreams. Suppose you wake up and are convinced you dreamt that you danced with wolves. Does that mean you dreamt you danced with wolves? It does, but only if you can distinguish between two different states: waking with the conviction of having dreamt of dancing with wolves even though you had no such dream versus waking with that conviction because you actually had the dream. An alternative source for such a conviction might be that you dreamt that you dined with a walrus but you misremembered, or misrecalled, or misinterpreted the experience as dancing with wolves. As dreams are rather insignificant on the whole, not much depends on the issue. However, exactly the same questions arise with respect to the interpretations that people, when fully conscious, put on experiences that they had when in a state of rapture or semiconsciousness.

The analogy to dreams raises another question. If one dreams of dances with wolves, one does not conclude that there were any wolves with which one actually danced. That conclusion is unaffected by the vividness of the dream. Why does a particularly vivid experience when meditating or praying deserve any special status? That is, if we do not deduce the existence of dancing wolves from dreams about dancing wolves, then we should not deduce the existence of God from some semiconscious state in which we appear to have had contact with Him. To treat the two experiences as having completely different consequences for one's conception of reality is to apply standards that, though they may keep some people happy, are neither Spartan nor merito-cratic. It is just arbitrariness.

It is precisely because of the failure of the argument from personal conviction of normal individuals that one is likely to encounter the argument from attestation of spiritual experts. For such experts have credentials that lend weight to their own intu-itions, where normal believers have only the strength of their convictions. So, consider now a covert spiritual expert, that is, one whose notoriety stems from an unusual ability rather than from self-professed saintliness.

First example: Uncle Morry

My example of a spiritual expert with an unusual ability is my 'uncle' Morris Tester. (In fact, Uncle Morry was my father's mother's first cousin.) He tells his story in *Hands That Heal*, an autobiography and account of his beliefs.[27] He was a chartered surveyor who became afflicted with a very severe back problem. My father, who, at the time, was training under him for his arti-cles, recalls how rapidly his situation worsened, how within months, he could only walk bent double, with sticks. Doctors told him that surgery was the only hope. However, back surgery in those days had an extremely low success rate. Understandably, he was desperate to find other means to recover his health.

The 'other means' came through a business associate, who asked him the simple question 'If I send you to somebody who could help you, will you go without asking silly questions?'. So, Morris Tester met Edward Fricker, a famous spiritual healer. There, two important things happened. He cured Uncle Morry's back problem – 'The family doctor, who made a routine call, was amazed to see me trotting around happily and even dancing a few carefree steps to a new LP' – and told him that he too could heal others. (It is important to note that a Wimpole Street specialist, who made diagnoses before and after the course of treatment by Fricker, was positive that the condition was not psychosomatic and could not have healed of its own accord.) In time, Morris Tester gave up his surveyor work and became a full time spiritual healer. Though he found 'the theology of orthodox religions' 'sterile and unacceptable', he was a strong adherent of 'the philosophy of Spiritualism', the 'only ... philosophy: trust God and live one day at a time'.

The argument that can be made for God's existence given people like Uncle Morry is very obvious. Uncle Morry had special abilities. His explanation of his abilities revolved crucially around God. His special abilities give his insights and beliefs a special status. So, if Uncle Morry believes in God, then God must exist.

The argument is slightly reminiscent of the argument involving Einstein. Crudely put: Einstein was special and believed in God, so God exists. Now, of course, the Einstein argument relies on the premise that everything Einstein believed was true, which is rather unconvincing. Uncle Morry's argument does not require the same assumption, because his belief in God is tied to his area of expertise (as was not the case with Einstein). We need only assume Uncle Morry's beliefs concerning his area of expertise correct. But is that assumption reasonable?

In a word: no. To see why Uncle Morry's argument is insufficient, consider a slightly altered version of the Einstein argument. Suppose that Einstein explained the source of his inspiration in physics by means of God – perhaps his insights arrived in a religious rapture that he felt to be Divine. Could we then argue that, because Einstein had special abilities that he felt revolved around God, we must be persuaded, as with Uncle Morry's intuitions, that God exists? This is hardly convincing, for having special mental abilities does not give one special insights into how the brain functions. What goes on inside the brain of a genius, or indeed inside anyone's brain, especially at the moment when ideas are conceived, is a matter of mystery. Just because one is particularly adept at conceiving ideas, it does not follow that one has special insight into the biology of thought. Einstein's genius is a thing entirely separate from Einstein's beliefs about the nature of Einstein's genius. Similarly, Uncle Morry's abilities are extraordinary, but they do not give him special qualifications in biology, so that he can tell, simply by introspection, what biological process take place when he does whatever it is that he does.

An analogy may make this simpler. The Mayans knew how to multiply numbers together.[28] Their procedure consisted in doubling and halving and tallying remainders. Yet, despite being convinced that the procedure worked, they had no mathematical explanation of *why* it worked. Instead, they developed a non-mathematical explanation, along the lines that the number two, and in consequence all even numbers, were evil and had to be removed from the calculation. Failure to remove them would corrupt the answer, that is, the wrong answer would result. Now, suppose yourself from a people that can add but cannot multiply. (To multiply seventeen by seven, you have to calculate seventeen plus seventeen plus seventeen plus seventeen plus seventeen plus seventeen plus seventeen.) You encounter the Mayans who inform you of their procedure for multiplying. By trying some examples, you convince yourself that the method works and you decide to adopt the Mayan procedure. Are you forced also to adopt the belief that the number two is evil? Naturally not. Just because Mayans have the special ability of multiplication, it does not follow that they have special insights into the process of multiplication. Similarly, just because Uncle Morry has special healing abilities, it does not follow that he has special insights into the mechanisms of his healing. His belief in God is no more reliable than the Mayans' belief in the evilness of the number two.

Second example: Paramahansa Yogananda

Paramahansa Yogananda is the late founder and leader of the Self-Realisation Fellowship, a worldwide organisation counting several thousand members, the aim of which is to disseminate the techniques of 'God realisation'. Drawing on Christianity and Hinduism, his brand of spiritualism belongs to the belief, ever increasing in popularity, that different religions are just different paths to the same God. Yogananda is an example of the second type of spiritual expert, who claims direct acquaintance with God and whose personal attestations convince some of God's existence. He writes, for instance, that, as a 'master ... of the mind, emotions, senses, passions', his 'actions ... are consonant with the will of God', that he is in 'God-communion', that he speaks 'not from book learning, but from perceptions of God': 'I could not speak of Him in this way if I didn't see or feel Him; He wouldn't let me'.[29] Are such claims evidence that God exists?

At first glance, nothing substantial differentiates Yogananda's personal convictions from anyone else's. I argued two sections earlier that a person's genuine and absolute conviction that they have had personal encounters with God does not amount to any evidence for God's existence. They are merely a personal interpretation of a personal experience. They are evidence of, rather than for, a prior conviction. The same applies to Yogananda's experiences.

Yet there remains the question of how one can be sure that Yogananda's personal interpretations of his personal experiences are not in fact the correct interpretations of those experiences. And, of course, the same question arises with respect to any spiritual expert of Yogananda's type. In the general case, studies such as Anthony Storr's, mentioned in Chapter 4, into the psychological make-up of self-proclaimed experts detract somewhat from the extent to which such people can seem convincing. The realisation that being the messenger of God, or in more extreme cases, being God proper, is merely a psychological 'template' detracts significantly from the sense of awe such self-proclaimers wish to engender. Indeed, the realisation demotes self-proclaimers from beings with other-worldly connections to individuals whose motives and mind are squarely rooted in this world.

The common thread that Storr reveals behind 'gurus' is that they are people of a particular ilk, who claim to know how they and others should live. Secondly, if good spiritual people, they often have a positive influence; if bad spiritual people, they often have a negative influence; if good scientifically-minded people, then they may found a new area of research and attract others to it; and so the list goes on, as the individual's nature and interests vary. Of course, returning such 'gurus', of whom spiritual experts are a subspecies, firmly to this world, one naturally expects that they will be subject to many of the human foibles that afflict us all. In other words, once one scrutinises spiritual experts, one finds that they often betray their limitations as mere members of this world. Yogananda is an excellent example of this.

He claims that his special relationship with God gives him access to all knowledge. Aware of this, I was interested to discover that the title of one of his essays was 'Reincarnation Can Be Scientifically Proven'. (Yogananda is very fond of the word 'scientific'. He discourses on the 'science of God-realisation' and has composed 'scientific affirmations'. His verses often use scientific allusion. In this, he is part of a curious tendency amongst religious people at large to appropriate the name of science in the hope of adding credence to creed. Science has not reciprocated.

The 'scientific proof' of reincarnation that Yogananda offers is meditation: 'Learn (1) to be conscious during sleep, (2) to be able to produce dreams at will, (3) to disconnect the five senses consciously, not unconsciously during sleep, and (4) to control the action of the heart, which is to experience conscious death, or the suspended animation of the body (but not of the consciousness) that occurs during the higher states of superconsciousness'.[30] Without having performed the requisite 'experiments', one is in no position to doubt Yogananda's, or other yogis', pronouncements. He reinforces this with an analogy: 'Germs are not visible to the naked eye; one must use a microscope to detect their presence. If a person refuses to look through the microscope, he cannot be said to have scientifically tested the theory that germs are present. His opinion is therefore valueless ... So it is in spiritual matters.' (A real example that Yogananda could have used is Cremonini's famous refusal to look through Galileo's telescope for fear of what he might see.)

The problem with this proof is that it is not scientific. Looking down a microscope is a good scientific way to discover germs because we are using something we already rely on, *viz.* vision, to explore something we do not, *viz.* germs. If someone looks down the microscope and sees nothing cell-like, then their vision can be tested. This alternative testing gives vision a measure of objectivity. Yogananda's proof, on the other hand, requires the development of a sixth sense. So, if someone does everything Yogananda instructs and then fails to perceive the reality of reincarnation, would that prove reincarnation a fiction, or would it undermine the proof by meditation? Yogananda would doubtless reject both alternatives, claiming instead that the practitioner was not yet advanced enough in meditation to judge whether reincarnation is real. But then there is no way to disagree with Yogananda: either you meditate and agree, or else he claims you have not meditated properly and have no right to disagree. In either case, the method of meditation lacks the checks to which vision is subject and, so, is unobjective and hence unscientific.

But the revelation of Yogananda's proof as spoof does not merely undermine his argument for reincarnation. It undercuts his claimed access to omniscience via God.[31] And this underlines the point I made at the outset of the discussion, that personal interpretations of personal experience, however convinced the experiencer is of their reality, guarantee nothing. I do not doubt that meditative and other rapturous or trance-like states, including 'tripping' and other drug-taking, create a very profound impression in the minds of those who experience them (a view based in part on my own experiences with meditation and in part on my lacking the requisite cynicism to dismiss outright the attestations of Yoganandas). However, the analogy with dreams and the errors of experts such as Yogananda undermine any theistic claims made on the basis of peculiar personal experiences.

Conclusion

I have been concerned primarily with two arguments. The first was a theoretical argument for the Spartan meritocracy's superiority over the Baroque monarchy and the corollary that atheism is superior to theism. The second was more practical, concentrating on the questions surrounding the good life, both in the ethical and the aesthetic sense of 'goodness'. Both these arguments support a worldview of which atheism is part.

In the last several sections, I have considered three different types of people whose existence might be considered to unsettle the conclusion of the two arguments just mentioned. These people were religious scientists and two types of what I called spiritual experts. The disquiet caused by theist scientists is that they practice both science and theism, which I had portrayed as fruits of diametrically opposed worldviews. If these intelligent people find no tension in such a position, then one might think that my position is missing something, or indeed is simply wrong. The disquiet caused by spiritual experts is that their claims concerning religious matters, most particularly the existence of God, superficially command respect and consideration enough to question the conclusion of the two central arguments of this book. However, I have argued in all these cases that personal beliefs of such people are, at best, irrelevant to an intellectually respectable defence of theism and, at worst, undermine it, potentially adding further support to atheism.

Chapter 6

Consequences: Religion and Government

Justice, justice shalt thou pursue – Deuteronomy 20:16

The will to believe

As stated in the Introduction, 'This book is about why atheism is correct, why theism is incorrect, and why anyone who cares about truth should be an atheist.' The preceding chapters have focused on two arguments for the superiority of atheism over theism. Presenting two different worldviews, the Spartan meritocracy and the Baroque monarchy, I argued that one, the meritocracy, is clearly sensible, that atheism is an instance of it, and that atheism in consequence makes sense; whereas I argued that the other, the monarchy, is nonsensical, that theism is an instance of it, and that theism in consequence makes no sense. The second argument showed how this superiority in theory translates into superiority in practice, with Sparta's successes standing in stark contrast to Baroque failures. So, the preceding chapters have focused on two arguments that speak to people who are concerned with truth, people for whom knowledge is more compelling than mere belief. However, not all people are so constituted.

Some people are driven by a simple will to believe. For such people, religion fulfils a basic desire to be religious. Their faith is impregnable to fact, their belief impervious to mere truth. They are capable of rejecting conclusions validly deduced from true premises whenever that conclusion contradicts tenets of their faith. Some are inclined to justify this position to some measure.

They cite, for instance, the unconsolingness of life when viewed as a scientific object, though they do not explain why 'non-consolingness' could not itself be a fact, a real facet of the world. Or they claim that religion or some other instance of the Baroque monarchy is essential to the human condition, a view against which I have already argued in the general case. Many propagators of the view that life without God is unconsoling would doubtless feel much less need for consolation if they did not so often declare themselves 'miserable wretches', 'unworthy sinners', 'wayward sheep', and so on. Others are probably not consoled by God, so much as they are disconcerted at the prospect of losing a long held 'companion', a remnant of childhood. But whatever the reasons for this unreason, such people exist and are impervious to arguments, which, like those presented above, strive after truth.

So, should this book, aimed as it is at 'anyone who cares about truth', be of no relevance to such people? Does it, and its arguments, hold nothing for them? The aim of this final chapter is to argue that the preceding chapters are indeed relevant to theists whose theism permits, or forces, them to reject the true, anti-theistic conclusions of valid arguments.

But before proceeding to that discussion, it must be made clear how much more than a mere reordering of priorities is at stake: truth over faith or faith before truth. Today's relativism makes differences of priorities seem entirely acceptable. However, the theist is not just reordering priorities, but rejecting a whole worldview. And I have been at pains to emphasise throughout the extreme success of that worldview. Just to take one part of its successes, consider the science and technology that have been deployed against polio. Surely, no one wishes to reject them. A simple reordering of priorities has huge knock-on effects in terms of the coherence of one's beliefs, on one's intellectual integrity. The challenge that besets the reprioritising theist is to explain how one can turn one's back on the worldview that, applied to the investigation of the world, yields the most successful set of explanations and applications that has ever been seen. (These arguments are presented at greater length in Chapter 3's *Ignoring Sparta* and briefly in Chapter 4's *Atheist Ethics*.)

Democracy and meritocracy

We live in a democracy, of sorts. In past ages, we were content to allow our values to be dictated by the church. We have learned, through hard experience, the necessity of cleaving church from state, of separating the two institutions and their powers. In our modern state of pluralism, the return to a joint church-state is made even harder. And yet religion continues to influence the government and its legislation, both directly and indirectly.

Religious institutions exercise direct influence on government through their representatives. The House of Lords in Britain, for example, contains various clergymen, including several bishops. And they exercise indirect influence through representation in quasi-governmental organisations and other bodies that the government consults when drafting policy. And further indirect influence arises through those members of parliament whose ethical outlook results from religious indoctrination, or education. Through all these channels, religions influence government and shape the law of the land.

Superficially, that is all well enough. We live, as said, in a democracy. People may freely associate themselves with a religious institution. And, if the institution has followers enough who defer in matters such as morals to the leaders of the organisation, then those leaders may speak as the voices of many. That is representation.

But that is only superficial. At the heart of the matter lie the principles that drive modern, pluralist democracies, those that drive religions, and the difference between them. And the difference is very great. Religions, as I have argued and repeated, are instances of Baroque monarchies. They compromise a set of stipulations to be accepted by the adherent, which no amount of subsequent contradiction or disrepute may discredit or displace. What is the nature of our democracy?

Fundamental to our society is the notion of freedom. And before freedom comes justice. Our laws aim to guarantee justice, freedom from persecution, freedom to pursue a life that is fulfilling and good. But freedom and justice are difficult notions (why else would philosophers be so intrigued by them?). It is not easy to say which of a variety of policies will best meet our aims of creating a free and just state. Obligations interact with freedom, justice interacts with freedom, and one form of freedom interacts with the next, and all this precipitates a string of accommodations and compromise. In heading towards our goal, therefore, we note two things. We cannot know in advance, absolutely and infallibly, what means will lead to our end. And, therefore, all means adopted are necessarily adopted provisionally, pending evidence of their good effect, with the possibility of later revision or rejection. These principles should be familiar, for they are meritocratic and Spartan respectively.

Democracy demands of us, therefore, that we base our laws on rational consideration of relevant evidence, that 'Policy-making ... be firmly based on analysis of what we know to be the facts'.[32] For how else will we find our way to ideals such as justice and freedom, given the complexity of the notions and the difficulty of the task? At heart, our state is, and must strive to be, a Spartan meritocracy. But this means that religion and our state are fundamentally in conflict: the principles that guide one are antithetical to those that guide the other.

So, returning to the questions that began this section, it is of course open to individuals to claim that, personally, they rank the pursuit of truth below the fabrication of consolation or the will to believe. There being no disputing about tastes, the matter rests there. However, when we leave the arena of the individual and enter the arena of the public, matters change substantially. Democracy demands reason and reasonableness. Its goals and ideals are conceivably achievable only through Spartan, meritocratic practice. This forces the censure of unreason. So, when the theist claims that we must legislate in a particular fashion, we must ask why, as our democratic duty. And any answer that ultimately comes to rest purely on a stipulation of some Baroque monarchy must be rejected.

So, the theory then is this. Democratic ideals, such as freedom and justice, are, in virtue of their complexity and ineffability, difficult to attain. They are, in consequence, best pursued by the principles of the Spartan meritocracy, by hardheaded trial and error and argument. Religion, being inherently non-Spartan and non-meritocratic, has no place within this process. Lacking as we do a clear line of vision to our target, religion is merely a stumbling block. Clerics in politics and religion in ethics are misplaced and unwelcome. This is underlined by the discussion of 'true' Christianity, or 'true' religion, in Chapter 4, where I argued that the text of any textually based religion has generally been compatible with so many mutually incompatible interpretations as to render both it and its exegetes incapable of providing society with a stable basis or steady direction. (Of course, a religious opinion can be subjected to the same process of rational evaluation with respect to democratic ideals. But then it is evaluated like any view. Its religious provenance is irrelevant, in particular, conferring no special status or worth on it.) It is our democratic duty to deny religion any undue influence over us in the pursuit of the ideals on which our society is founded. The influence of religious institutions on government, whether direct or indirect, is wrong. It is antidemocratic. In the attempt to achieve justice and freedom and, in short, democracy, issues of such importance are at stake that we cannot afford to leave them in the grasp of stipulation, unreason, and religion.

Case studies

How do these theoretical arguments fare in the face of reality? To answer this question, I will present four case studies. These will show how the pursuit of democratic ideals has been consistently hindered by religious institutions in the past, and how it continues to be so impeded in the present. But this claim is very easily misstated and even more easily misunderstood. So, I formulate it more carefully, before showing the relevance of the case studies to the issue.

Religions, by their monarchic nature, pursue a set of ideals, which are good, or at least holy, by definition. These values, if clerics are to be believed, are immutable truths, stemming from God or His spokesmen and -women. Yet, in reality they are highly mutable. They mutate as a result of trends in society. As society's perception and knowledge shift, its values move too. Correspondingly, what individuals believe to be good, right and proper changes. Individuals inclined to attribute a divine nature to their moral code project their new morality into their inter- pretation of the Bible or other holy writ. How does this affect religion?

In terms of personal religion, the changes can be drastic, as was the case in the pre-sixties and post-sixties generations: the younger people incorporated ideals of love, peace, harmony, toler- ance, into their moral outlook, ideals that were far less pronounced in the older generation and these ideals were equally manifest in sixties-style spiritualism. In terms of institutional religion, the changes are subtler. Institutions move with the times, at times. Often, however, moral movement is perceived as moral decline, necessarily so if the perceivers perceive them- selves to be at the pinnacle of morality: any move away from a pinnacle is a descent. In these circumstances, resistance results, and the resistance may not be overcome until the younger gener- ation supplants the older one within the institution. At that point, the younger moral outlook, somewhat matured, supplants the older, just in time for the process to begin again.

What we expect, then, is that religious sentiment should lead simultaneously to the supporting and rejection of almost any new view as religious sentiment will be married to both sides. (This relates to the earlier observation that there are good people and bad people and there are religious people and non-religious people, and the two are 'orthogonal', that neither religion nor religious sentiment is necessary for moral conduct, nor are they by any means sufficient.) If this is so, then we are right to reject religion from the engine of our society. We attempt to orientate ourselves so as best to reach democratic goals, a balance of justice, freedom and obligation. What value, in our search, is religious sentiment, a compass with two needles that always point in opposite directions?

The argument then is not that religion is a litmus test of democratic progress: whenever it shows red, we go. Rather it is that religious sentiment is irrelevant to any debate because it plays on both sides. However, where religious sentiment combines with institutional conservatism, it is almost sure to impede progress and is to be shunned.

In relation to these claims, I will consider three past cases: the abolition of slavery, the suffrage of women, and the emancipation of Jews. All these must be regarded as fundamental to the nature of modern, pluralist democracy, for we can hardly imagine calling ourselves just if we permitted slavery, or denied people the vote on the basis of gender or religion. In each case, however, we find religious sentiment on both sides of debate and religious institutions most often set against reform. Before examining each case, let me note why I have chosen these three. Slavery is included because it is here that religion has the greatest cause for pride. Suffrage is included because of the importance of its result: the contribution of women to society generally and to politics in particular would have been impossible without it. Jewish emancipation is included as an instance of minority rights, though much the same purpose could have been served by the discussion of its precursor, emancipation of Christians, irrespective of denomination.[33]

Case one: slavery and its abolition

Slavery and the slave trade did not merely engender inhumanity; lack of humanity was prerequisite to them. The story of the abolition movement[34] is the story of the gradual widening of eyes and minds in slave trading countries: eyes had to be opened to the cruelty of the slave trade, minds broadened to allow blacks dignity as humans, the possible objects of brotherly love. In England, opposition to slavery, amongst both populace and politicians, was often the manifestation of the deeply Christian sentiments of deeply Christian people. And anti-abolitionists were often dependent on slavery for their wealth and power, either directly, as slave traders, or indirectly, as traders in slave produce, such as sugar, or as political representatives of ports, such as London and Liverpool, dependent on slave-based commerce. Thus simplified, we see an instance of money as the root of all evil: on one side, mercantile ambition in support of an evil; on the other, Christianity against it. As slavery is an anathema to our modern (democratic) sentiments, does the good work of Christians in this cause contradict the claim that the pursuit of democratic ideals is better off without divines' intervention?

The short answer is: no. But the grounds for asserting this are rather tangled. The first body of relevant facts comes from the nature of Christian opposition to slavery, which took a very long time to embrace the idea that slavery *per se* was wrong. The second body comes from Christianity's relationship with slavery over several centuries, in particular prior to 1750.

The opening paragraph's portrayal of the end of slavery had abolition as by and large an ethical affair and anti-abolition as by and large an economic one. Though not inaccurate as a representation of modern preconceptions, the truth is, as always, more complex. Both sides marshalled ethical, economic and religious arguments. The appearance of religious conviction on both sides of the debate is what I claimed was to be expected: 'the argument is that religious sentiment is irrelevant because it plays on both sides'. In fact, religious sentiment was for a long time perfectly content with slavery or even actively encouraged it. Criticism of slavery was rare, and when it did occur, was generally directed at mere aspects of its practice. Though this case cannot be made in detail here, a few indications of its correctness can be given.

Religion was often partial justification for slavery. For instance, Louis XIII's initial resistance to the slave trade was overcome by the prospect that *négriers* would save the unfortunate Africans from their paganism by bringing them into the way of Christ[35]; whereas in England until around 1750, lively debate surrounded the theological justification for converting slaves. A simplified theology, suitable to their inferior intellects, would help fashion the blacks' obedience and servility.[36] (This was true in isolated cases. James Walvin cites one in which slave owner and slaves all converted to evangelical Christianity. The owner reported an increase in productivity and decrease in disciplinary difficulties.) Or religion was used to bring critics of slavery to heel, as in 1642, when the Protestant synod at Rouen reproached 'over-scrupulous persons who thought it unlawful for Protestant merchants to deal in slaves'. Likewise, when Anthony Benezet urged the Society for the Propagation of the Gospel to abandon slavery, they replied, 'Though the Society is fully satisfied that your intention in this matter is perfectly good, yet they most earnestly beg you not to go further in publishing your notions, but rather to retract them ...'[37].

There was religious criticism of the slave trade early on. Total condemnation came from Catholics and Quakers. The Vatican objected intermittently but was rarely heeded. The Inquisition, Catholicism's most active body, was more concerned with claims that specific slave traders were secret Jews than with slave welfare, despite Pope Clement XI's urging an end to slavery. Papal efforts had little concrete effect beyond leading Philip III, King of Spain and Portugal, to decree that all slave trading vessels must carry a priest. Nor did Quaker attempts achieve much. Indeed, George Fox, the founder Quaker, who preached brotherhood to the slave owners of the West Indies and denounced slavery in Barbados, himself owned slaves in Pennsylvania.

But blanket criticism of slavery from religious quarters was rare until the religious revivals began. More common was partial criticism. For instance, António Vieira, the great preacher, opposed slavery of Amazonian Indians, but not of Africans. Indeed, like Las Casas, a century and a half before, he urged

African slavery as a remedy for the labour shortages that led to the enslaving of Indians. Others, like Germain Fromageu, a theologian who presided over a tribunal for cases of conscience, denounced the common practice of kidnapping Africans for slaves: the proper source of slaves was captives in war. And, Reverend Richard Saltonstall denounced merely 'the act of stealing negers, or of taking them by force ... *on the Sabbath Day*' as contrary to God's law.[38]

Even when the eighteenth century's religious revival began and slaves came to Jesus in droves, religious advocacy of the slaves' case was predicated on fellow feeling towards Christians, not on fellowship with humans beings. And before slaves became co-religionists with revivalists, protests were isolated and neglected, 'individual actions by unrepresentative people'.

A more characteristic reaction was that of some Baptists in South Carolina who wrote home to England to ask for guidance as to how to treat a brother member of their Church who had castrated a slave. They received the reply that they should not risk dissension in the movement over 'light or indifferent causes'.[39]

Indeed, there is 'no record in the seventeenth century of any preacher who, in any sermon, whether in the Cathedral of Saint-André in Bordeaux, or in a Presbyterian meeting house in Liverpool, condemned the trade in black slaves'.[40]

Such, then, was the role of religion in abolition. Against the leadership of good Christians, such as William Wilberforce, must be weighed the religion's encouragement of slavery, both in providing it with justification and in silencing its opposers. Against revivalists' fervent feeling for fellow Christians must be weighed their lack of feeling for fellow humans. Moreover, against both of these must be weighed the contribution of rationalists and humanists to the climate of abolitionist sentiment, which I now briefly outline.

Among those who paved the way for the abolitionist movement, Aphra Behn was particularly significant. Hugh Thomas claims that her contribution 'can scarcely be exaggerated', that she was 'more influential than popes and missionaries'.[41] Her contribution was the presentation of a *humanitarian* case against slavery, most famously in her 1688 publication, *Oroonoko, or the History of the Royal Slave*, which was to begin to open eyes and minds to the plight and rights of slaves.

Humanist ideals were part of a whole raft of Enlightenment philosophy, and sentiment, whose leaders included Voltaire, Montesquieu, Marivaux, Diderot, and Rousseau. All were critics of slavery. In Diderot's famous *Encyclopedia or Reasoned Dictionary of the Sciences*, Louis de Jaucourt wrote that slavery 'violates religion, morality, natural law, and all human rights'. Anti-slavery was firmly part of Enlightenment ideas, as was *fraternité*, which, amongst revivalists, was known as 'brotherly love'.

Besides Enlightenment thought, another rationalist French philosophy was opposed to slavery. Cartesianism, as explained in Chapter 1, held, on non-dogmatic grounds, that the world was divided into two substances, the spiritual and physical. It was a consequence of Cartesian philosophy that blacks, far from being inferior, shared with Europeans 'rational souls' and all their co-attendant dignity. Recall that all physical phenomena were supposed to be mechanical, and so reducible to geometry. Language use was not reducible to geometry and, so, could only exist in the presence of something non-physical, that is, a soul. In consequence, all speaking things had souls. Africans spoke. Therefore, they had souls. Moreover, spiritual substance did not come in different 'degrees' or 'levels of purity', so there was no claiming that Africans had inferior souls. Their souls gave them the dignity of the Divine. One finds clear evidence of this Cartesian influence in, for instance, Dr Thomas Aubrey's biographical work, *The Sea Surgeon, or the Guinea Man's Vademecum*, which appeared in 1729: 'For, though they are heathens, yet they have a rational soul as well as us; and God knows whether it may not be more tolerable for them in the latter day [of Judgement] than for many who profess themselves Christians.'

Thus, rationalist philosophy and humanist ideology played a significant part in the battle against slavery by helping to create a climate of ideas which permitted empathy with Africans and hostility to the inhumanity of their mistreatment. Though it is hard to quantify to what extent these ideas were responsible for the shift in attitudes that was prerequisite for the abolitionist movement, it is certain that the movement was far from free from their influence.

We can now return to the relationship between religion and politics, which is the theme of this chapter. The claim is that religion proceeds according to principles antithetical to those that must guide the pursuit of democratic ideals (Baroque and monarchic versus Spartan and meritocratic) and, hence, that religious sentiment *per se* should always be ignored in the pursuit of democratic ideals. This sounds well in theory, but would it have worked in practice? Would listening to religion have expedited or impeded fundamental moves towards democratic ideals of justice and freedom?

In this context, I turned to the abolition of slavery, in which religion played a well-known role. In reality, religion was found on both sides of the debate, providing justification both for slavery and for its abolition. Often it merely straddled the fence, impassive or indifferent. And when religion really rallied against slavery, much of the ideological battle had already been fought by rationalist, non-religious forces. This is not meant to belittle the contribution of the religious, which was very great. Rather, it reveals that religion and abolition were very much different concerns, and that both interacted strongly with rational philosophies of the time. The marked religious involvement in the abolition of slavery does not prove that the pursuit of democratic ideals would have been served by heeding the religious voice, for this ignores the contradictory voices that laid claim to religious justification and it ignores the partially non-religious origin of the ideas that the religious came to advocate.

Case two: Jewish emancipation

Fundamental to a pluralist society is the protection of minorities, especially when those minorities are not large enough to make any politician's future dependent on their good will and votes. In securing such protection, the state has often first had to protect the minority from the state itself. This was the case with Jewish emancipation. The case of Jews is suited to the present examination of religion and democratic progress in two respects: as a general case, it illustrates the path towards the abolition of (baseless) discrimination, and, as a particular case, it concerns a minority that has made great contributions, not least in the political sphere, where the debate concerning Jewish 'disabilities' and 'relief' originally raged. What forces fought for, and against, a cause so important, both ideologically and practically, to our modern democracy? In particular, what was the role of religion and the religious?

Jewish relief was symbolic above all, for Jews were too small a minority to compel politicians to act in their interest. The symbolic nature of the debate centred on the character of the nation, of its constitution, and of its government. What gave the debate much impetus was, however, an entirely practical affair: whether a Jew – generally a particular Jew, Lionel de Rothschild – properly elected by the people, should be allowed to take his seat in Parliament. The affair remained politically active over a sustained period. Fourteen Jewish relief bills were introduced to Parliament. The first foundered in the House of Commons and, of the remaining thirteen, the House of Lords rejected all that received a majority in the lower House. This resistance continued, notwithstanding *The First Report of Her Majesty's Commissioners for Revising and Consolidating the Criminal Law*, which, in 1845, concluded that 'the ancient laws affecting Jews arose out of institutions of a barbarous period, equally opposed to good policy, justice and humanity'.[42] It is almost needless to say that our modern laws strive to create and uphold 'good policy, justice and humanity'. What arguments and sentiments led to the fourteen-fold frustration of these three democratic principles and to the perpetuation of 'barbarous' laws that denied 'the right of the Hebrew people to enjoy equal civil privileges with their Christian neighbours'?[43]

The conservative position was a combination of religion, constitutional doctrine, and populism. Parliament had only recently conceded its purely Protestant composition. In severing the link between Anglicanism and government, it could be satisfied with the compromise that Parliament remained at least a Christian body, all of whose members swore a Christian oath before assuming their seats. The possible disappearance of the Christian compromise aroused strong sentiments. Opponents of reform regarded the battle against Jewish relief as a last stand: they 'warned repeatedly that admitting the Jew would open the way to the "Hindoo", the "Parsee" and the "votary of Boodh" '.[44]

A misconception then prevalent, and still popular, was that Jesus was the fount of morality, the foundation of civil society. To such people, the possible de-Christianising of government was a threat to morality itself, the bedrock of society. One such adherent, W.J. Conybearne, saw in the 'Judaising [of] parliament' the embodiment of the principle that 'government has nothing to do with religion or morality'.[45] With the very fabric of society at stake, Sir Frederic Thesiger warned against defying the convictions and sensibilities of the masses: 'the greatest violence to the religious sentiments and feelings of the nation' would follow 'if the House admitted Jews by removing the requirement of a Christian oath'.[46] Thesiger probably did not misjudge the common man's lack of fellow feeling towards the Jew. Jews numbered only a few thousand and were concentrated in the main trading cities. The opportunity to contradict and dispel the distilled bigotry of centuries was, therefore, not available to most.

Such, then, was the opposition to Jewish relief: at some times religious-cum-constitutional, at others, religious-cum-populist, and at yet others, religious pure and simple. Each of these attacks was met by the pro-reformists. For instance, with regard to the constitution, one can note the parliamentary debate of April 25, 1848, in which the Earl of St Germain stated that, in England, 'all natural-born subjects had the same legal rights' and Lord Brougham delivered what amounted to a lecture on 'the doctrine of the constitution'.[47] With regard to the will of the people, the radical Raikes Currie denounced the 'obstinate resistance on the part of the Lords to the now emphatically declared will of the people of England'.[48] And, in the same 1848 debate, Lord Russell, prime minister and protagonist in the parliamentary struggle for Jewish relief, affirmed the role of religion in public and private life and implied that resistance to relief evidenced a want of Christianity. As with previous bills, the Lords rejected the one debated in and around April 1848, by 163 votes to 128.

'Jewish emancipation,' writes David Feldman, 'was a step within a larger process extending civil and political liberties through society.'[49] In this march of the ideals that lie at the heart of our pluralist society, did religion feed or impede progress? To be sure, some proponents of reform did attempt to marshal religious sentiment. However, religion seems to have been heavily against sweeping away old laws that hindered 'good policy, justice and humanity'. Religion was the heart of constitutional arguments for conservatism, the heart of populist arguments for the status quo, and the heart of the moral and moderately nationalist arguments for perpetuating inequality. And yet the case of Jewish emancipation was fundamental to modern society in many respects: as part of 'a larger process extending civil and political liberties through society', as part of the struggle for minority rights in general, and as the necessary first step that enabled the Jewish minority to contribute greatly to our society. The present case, therefore, supports the current claim that, in the pursuit of our democratic ideals, religion is more likely to lead us astray than not.

Case three: female suffrage

Lord Shaftesbury, who, as a younger man, had been vigorous in the pursuit of abolition, spoke out strongly against Jewish emancipation in his later life. He warned his fellow politicians that they had already conceded the Protestant Parliament, accepting instead a merely Christian one. If they conceded that too, the day would come when they would have to fight even for the male Parliament.[50] Lord Shaftesbury, right as he was, provides a neat bridge from the first and second to the last past case, namely, female suffrage.

As before, the focus here is on the relationship between religion and a movement fundamental to our democracy – both theoretically, in its effect on our conception of justice and equality, and practically, in its impact on the political and economic spheres and on family life. As before, religion was to be found on both sides of the argument. So, at best, the current case proves that religious sentiment is unrevealing of how to achieve democratic ideals. Yet, the case is more complex and more curious; for religious support of female suffrage very often rejected, at least tacitly, the principle of equality which it seems to us to represent. Female suffrage was not the realisation of a great ideal, democratic or religious. It was merely an expediency, a lesser evil. So, though religion fought for and against suffrage, its support of suffrage was only coincidentally coincident with democratic ideology.

The anti-suffragist case was a complex one. The full phalanx of arguments comprised not only religious opinion, but 'political, medical, psychological, sociological, imperialist, military and philanthropic'[51] opinions too, as well as a strong strand of anti-intellectualism. Religious rhetoric and sentiment were common. For instance, the anti-suffragists Herbert Ryle and Hensley Henson showed a ' "cross-bench mentality" in religion'.[52] Quotations from Genesis and St Paul made appearances, but more common were sentiments like Earl Percy's: 'The real fact is that man in the beginning was ordained to rule over the woman,' he said in the 1873 suffrage debate, 'and this is an Eternal decree which we have no right and no power to alter'.[53]

Earl Percy's sentiments were echoed in Mrs Frederic Harrison's elegant and eloquent attack on suffrage, *The Freedom of Women*, which appeared in 1908. (Mrs Harrison's pamphlet includes nearly all of the arguments mentioned above, and, through its excellent structure and clarity, must rather have undercut claims, like Sir Edward Clarke's, also in 1908, that female suffrage would dangerously increase the electorate's irresponsibility, lack of education, and preoccupation with personality.) Mrs Harrison clearly regarded religion, and not just Christianity, as providing a strong anti-suffragist argument.

> Politicians and legists have but followed in the track of the great religious systems of the past ; often the religious teacher has been the law-giver as well. The great religions of the East, with their more or less cloistered women, taught the duty of the submission and the true subjection of women. Mahomet, while seeking to protect women, assigned to them an inferior position in this world and the next, and imposed upon them a rigid rule. Under the Jewish Dispensation women were taught that they had brought sin and sorrow into the world, which they hardly expiated as the child-bearers of the race.
>
> Early Christianity inherited the tradition of Eve, mother of mankind, and with that tradition a profound mistrust of the female sex. ... The extraordinary contributions of women to the Church, however, gradually raised their position and their estimation in ecclesiastical eyes—an estimation which culminated in the uplifting of the Virgin Mother for the adoration of mankind.[54]

Indeed, she even chose to end her pamphlet with a religious allusion: 'It seems to us that in taking the vote women will be selling their birthright for a mess of pottage.'

The influence of religion went beyond overtly religious arguments, however. This can be seen, for instance, in the willingness to substitute 'Nature' for 'God' in various anti-suffragist arguments, as in 'the Antis' central belief that a separation of spheres between the sexes had been ordained by God and/or by Nature'.[55] This rather Spinozan tendency was part of a wider non-theistic repackaging of certain old Church beliefs, in particular those that were flattering to man. Another example concerned man's being master of the field, a phrase interpreted by some as meaning that

God had made man's mind capable of unravelling all the mysteries of the universe. As with all theology, one can hardly see what determines that as true or false. However, and rather remarkably, the same view was later reformulated as Nature having ensured that man's mind would understand all her mysteries. This view was, of course, hardly scientific, relying, as it did, on a teleological conception of nature and an anthropomorphic turn of phrase. Perhaps men were reluctant to relinquish what religion had taught them was their special status. Whatever the explanation, it must be appreciated that such apparently non-theistic views as a Nature-ordained separation of spheres in reality owed much to theology.

In this small space, it is impossible to catalogue at length the full variety of religious opposition to female suffrage and the preceding paragraphs must be taken as indicative of a much broader picture, in which religion was not only directly part of the attack on suffragism, but was also the subtle source of other prongs of the same case against the freedom of women.

But what of religious support of suffragism? It was both hardy and half-hearted. This peculiar combination is best illustrated by events in North America. The modern movement for female suffrage began in 1869 in the East, which was, naturally, where cosmopolitan and political ideas first landed. Within little more than a year, two territories had enacted female suffrage. Yet these trail-blazers were both remote and primitive parts of the West: Wyoming Territory and the Mormon Territory of Utah. This is, of course, surprising – most preconceptions would have these areas as backward in how they regard and treat women. So, are the preconceptions wrong, or were there other factors at play?

Certainly, initially, religious opinion was largely set against female suffrage. 'In fact, by the late nineteenth century that movement was seen as anathema by many who claimed to be religious and it increasingly relied on rationalistic rather than religious arguments to make its cause.'[56] This situation changed largely because of the tenacity and energy of people such as

Olympia Brown, a minister and preacher, to whose religious worldview suffrage was central.

However, to understand the actual enactment of female suffrage, one must look beyond religious conscience and into political reality. What was key, writes Alan Grimes, was 'who in America thought they would gain power if women voted, and who thought they would lose power'.[57] He argues that, at least in the West, female suffrage was politically expedient: 'the constituency granting woman suffrage was composed of those who also supported prohibition and immigration restriction and felt woman suffrage would further their enactment'.[58] As a rule, suffrage was part of the platform of smaller parties, ones that needed all the support they could muster. What emerges, then, is a picture in which women were not granted the vote because it was the right thing to do. Indeed, as the preceding paragraph illustrates, it was often felt as the wrong thing to do. Rather, it was a lesser evil, a necessary compromise on the road to religious goals.

Lessons from the past

The purpose of examining abolition, emancipation and suffrage has been to see how a particular theoretical argument plays out in practice. The theoretical argument concerns the role that we should permit religion to play in the politics and legislative processes of a pluralist democracy such as ours. Fundamental to any democracy is the pursuit of democratic ideals such as equality, justice, freedom tempered by obligation. Difficult concepts, they are difficult to achieve and the best way ahead must recognise the likelihood of failure and the constant need for revision, may make no single policy unrevisable or unrejectable, and must base its decision making procedure on careful consideration of the relevant facts. That is, the best way ahead is both Spartan and meritocratic. And if democracy is Spartan and meritocratic, then, by the arguments of the first chapter, it is also atheist. Now, this does not mean that atheism should be enforced on every individual. Rather, the *mechanisms* of democracy – the legislative procedure, etc. – should be atheist, being Spartan and meritocratic. Conversely, by the arguments of the first chapters, religion is un-Spartan and anti-meritocratic. And, consequently, the democratic machinery should remain free from religion: religious sentiment must be recognised as irrelevant to the creation of good democratic laws; religious beliefs should have no platform in governing bodies; religious creed may not be enshrined in law, except where it coincides with democratic interests. Democracy proceeds by one set of principles. Religion by the opposite. To mix the two is to allow into the heart of democracy fundamentally antidemocratic forces.

In examining the changing circumstances of slaves, Jews and women, the purpose was to find evidence of fundamental differences between democracy and religion, and of the inappropriateness of allowing the latter to lead the former. Now, both religion and democracy are supposed to be able to tell us how to live. And the abolition of slavery, the emancipation of minorities, and the equality of women are of paramount importance to the nature of just, pluralist democracy. However, they seem hardly to have been so central to the realisation of religious ideals. If religious interest had exactly coincided with democratic progress, then there would have been a strong case for allowing religion a substantial role in our politics. If religion and democracy had always taken exactly opposite views, then we could have been sure that the two at least had similar views about what constitute key issues. However, in all of the cases above, democratic ideals simply split religious sentiment: theology and fervent theistic feeling fell on both sides of every argument. In other words, the pursuit of democratic ideals has nothing to gain from religion because religious feeling is simultaneously compatible with both sides of debates of the most fundamental importance to democracy.

And yet, even when democracy and religion converge on a single goal, they often do so for very different reasons. So, religious support of abolition was often predicated on fellow feeling for Christian brothers. In modern democratic thought, slavery is wrong in virtue of a more basic brotherhood: faith-free fraternity, which embraces all people simply because they are people. Likewise, religious support for female suffrage was sometimes straightforward, as with Olympia Brown and her followers. However, often it was merely a way to wage war on other fronts: on immigration and alcohol.

The ambivalence of the religious voice in matters of paramount importance on the path to democracy and the coincidental nature of their convergence both underline the theoretical argument summarised above: there is no place for religion in the democratic machinery by which we pursue democratic ideals. To attempt to heed religion in such circumstances is like trying to find one's way out of a mountain pass by obeying the command 'Come this way!' while it echoes off every cliff and precipice.

On the rifeness of unreason

I would now like to illustrate the issues outlined above in their current context. For, even though reason and reasonableness are the only ways likely to bring us closer to ideals of justice, equality, freedom, and so on, yet unreason remains rife in government, politics, and public fora. The very armaments and arguments of the anti-abolitionists, of the anti-emancipationists, and of the anti-suffragists are still heard today, whenever any of several topics are raised in Parliament or in the media. As homosexuality is in the media again at the time of writing, it will serve my purpose in this section. Judging things by my own lights, I would have chosen another topic, thinking homosexuality an issue of relative unimportance to the public in general. However, its propensity to provoke such passionate debate assures me that it is an abiding public interest and therefore warrants proper, reasoned treatment. In particular, arguments deployed against the fundamentals of democracy must be recognised when they re-emerge in order to be viewed for what they are.

For concreteness, I will consider a specific law, Section 28, which forbids local government authorities from promoting homosexuality in schools and which the New Labour government has undertaken to repeal the legislation, against the will of many. Below, I will argue, firstly, that the legislation ought to be repealed. This then allows me to address the arguments against change. I will show that they are not new arguments. Indeed, there is little to suggest that they have anything to do with homosexuality *per se*. Rather, they are generic buttresses for the status quo, having served against each of the three reform movements examined above. To allow ourselves to be misguided by these old enemies of democracy – of justice, of equality, of freedom – is to neglect our duty as citizens of a democratic state.

Clearly, there are ways of interpreting 'promotion' that make the promotion of homosexuality wrong – for instance, if promotion were to involve large scale indoctrination. However, there are much subtler ways of promotion and these include things as simple as telling the truth. Let me illustrate a few of these from personal experience.

At Sunday lunch a little while ago, I, as the guest scientist, was asked by the hosts' sixteen-year-old daughter why some people think homosexuality to be (partly) genetically determined, if homosexuals, as is often assumed, generally do not pass on their genes to offspring. I answered by using some WHO statistics concerning a condition that appears to be genetic, but which cannot generally be passed on directly because people with the condition rarely reproduce. How can such conditions exist, she wanted to know? I gave a simplified, possibly oversimplified, analogy of two brown-eyed parents producing blue-eyed children, because I remembered having had that example myself at school and thought it might still be used today.

But was homosexuality natural? It is common in the natural world, as numerous studies of animal behaviour have revealed. Indeed, some species apparently have homosexual courtship behaviour distinct from heterosexual courtship. If experts in nature keep on discovering instances of it in the natural world, then I suppose it is natural. And then there are studies that correlate sexuality with physical characteristics, such as brain shape, auditory sensitivity, and, in a recent eyebrow raiser, finger length. No, that was not what she meant by natural; it was more, what's the point of homosexuality? One possibility is that homosexuality gives the evolutionary edge to small communities, as could have existed amongst human hunter-gatherers – another phrase I remembered hearing at school. There was a study of foxes that showed some of the relevant points. Then dessert arrived and no one was interested in talking for a while.

The next day, it occurred to me to wonder whether a biology teacher at school could say what I had said. I had told an adolescent that homosexuality was natural and may have been important in our evolutionary history. I had not said it was right, but I doubt she will ever believe the 'homosexuality is wrong because unnatural' argument. And that is not far off promoting homosexuality. Yet another thing I recall (over)hearing at school was a teacher telling off someone in the year below me for calling one of his classmates a freak. The teacher told him, in a nutshell, that what he had said was wrong morally and, in the current case, was wrong factually, too: the former, because bullying hurts people, and the latter, because homosexuality is natural. Both those things are true, but would saying the second constitute promotion of homosexuality? In both these cases, homosexuality was being promoted, not by having its practice advocated, but more subtly, by forming attitudes towards those who practise it.

Not promoting homosexuality can clash with mere truth telling in other ways. My first school was Presbyterian. I was one of only two Jews in my year and, for most of the time, the only one in my class. The school could hardly be called anti-Semitic, though it still left plenty of room for anti-Semitic incidents. Initially, I found such incidents bewildering. Only when I realised what they were about did they become hurtful. I did not feel ashamed of being a Jew; I just kept quiet. Then one day, Mr Spencer – Mr Chips in disguise – mentioned that some hero of history was a Jew. Suddenly, and for the first time, being a Jew was something to be proud of. And, though the class' only Jew, I was not the only one affected by the news. It had an effect on my self-regard and on others' behaviour, if, perhaps, only temporarily. On reflection, this was promotion of Judaism, not by advocating its practice, but, again, by forming attitudes towards those who practise, or have practised, it.

Of course, one can imagine a similar incident occurring today in similar circumstances, but with Alan Turing the homosexual substituted for someone-or-other the Jew. To mention sexual orientation would once again be only to tell the truth and would certainly be no more gratuitous than mentioning religion. As in my story, it could even have a positive effect, either on self-perception or other perception. Yet here again, to tell the truth is to break the law. A Ukrainian friend remembers that her communist school books taught that Popov had invented the radio, Yablochkin, the lightbulb – promoting Western values, even by praising those who had 'practised' them, was prohibited. Clearly, we are far from that. But both raise the same question: what has gone wrong when telling the truth is wrong, when telling the truth is no longer an uncompromised goal of education?

Truth is not the sole goal of education: moral and mental maturity are too. Yet, the problems with Section 28 extend to this domain today. Homosexual and bisexual youth suffer from feelings of isolation. This is hardly surprising: the norm is the expectation and heterosexuality is the norm. In addition to the difficulty of not feeling normal, there is the common opposition to non-heterosexuality, and its vilification. The general climate does not lead young homosexuals to expect a positive reaction if they try to broach the subject. By giving schools and teachers adequate power and information, this situation could be ameliorated. Yet, forty percent of teachers have been approached by homosexual and bisexual students for advice, and over fifty percent of teachers report difficulty in meeting students' needs because they are concerned about Section 28. Charities for the young, such as Childline and the National Children's Bureau, support the repeal of the Act, as do medical organisations and the

National Union of Teachers.[59] So, Section 28 is the opposite of everything that a healthy education should aim for: truth, morality, and maturity.

What is the case then against repeal? It consists of many elements, every one of them witnessed in the battles against abolition, minority emancipation, and equal suffrage. These range from the abstract, such as the symbolic value of legislation, through the practical, such as the way to ensure the moral health of society, down to the derisive and prejudiced.

Margaret Thatcher's correct observation that laws 'have a symbolic significance: they are signposts to the way society is developing – and the way the legislators of society envisage that it should develop'[60] recalls earlier incidents: Feldman's statement that 'the issue of Jewish disabilities was primarily symbolic',[61] Asquith's labeling female suffrage 'a travesty of democratic institutions'.[62] What is symbolically at stake is the connection between morality and government. So, Thatcher regards the gay activism as part of a movement, beginning in the 1960s and resulting in 'an almost complete separation between traditional Christian values and the authority of the state'.[63] Yet, the debate for Jewish emancipation was already regarded as the last line of defense for the connection between religion and state. Recall W.J. Conybearne's warning of 1847: 'the principle, which is to receive its final triumph and complete development in a Judaising parliament, is that the end of government has nothing to do with religion or morality'. Similar sentiments concerning suffrage have been cited above.

In enlisting morality against change, the implicit argument is that failure to reform is a minor injustice, one necessary for the health of the whole. So, the Home Secretary, Lord North, though he accepted the spirit of Sir Cecil Wray's abolitionist amendment to a more moderate bill of 1783, regretted that the trade was 'necessary to every country in Europe'.[64] Likewise, Curzon declared to cheers in 1912: 'If the interests of women were opposed to the interests of the State, then I say fearlessly the interests of the State must prevail.'[65] Jewish disabilities were similarly justified. In the case of homosexuals, the injustices are deemed necessary to protect children from exploitation and to protect the family from further erosion. Exactly these arguments were deployed against female suffrage.

Both in case of women and homosexuals, the arguments are clearly misguided. First, consider women: the modern 'crisis of the family' certainly followed female suffrage. But did it follow *from* that change? The sizeable delay between the two makes suffrage an unlikely cause. Far more important were two inventions: the washing machine and the pill. Household appliances gave women more time, the pill gave them more control over that time. Only with these in hand could women have realistic aspirations to a life beyond the home and only once these aspirations existed could the rebellion against the traditional family begin. Those who advocate a return to old values must first effect a return to old technology. Second, consider homosexuals. The protection of children demands the repeal of Section 28, for the reasons given above. And the only family that is under attack from continued expansion of gay rights is the Victorian vision of family bliss, where grandparents are mere guests and cousins, an intrusion. To the many, including me, for whom family crucially includes not only grandparents, cousins, uncles and aunts, but also second and third cousins, great uncles and aunts, and so on, the nuclear family seems dysfunctional. And whether homosexuals are part of families, in the organic extended not Victorian topiaried sense, is a factual question. Certainly, Mrs Frederic Harrison's notion of family embraces homosexuals, where 'the new generation learns to appreciate the continuity of the race, comes to feel gratitude for the noble inheritance bequeathed to every human son and daughter from the past, and feels the desire to hand it on undiminished and untarnished to the future'.[66] The family values argument is fodder for reform rather than resistance.

And then there is the less thinking side of the debate. Abolitionists were, for a period, mostly an intellectual minority, such as the Enlightenment's leaders, Voltaire, Diderot,

Montesquieu. Pro-Jewish reformers were likewise part of an intellectually driven reform movement. And suffragist literature could be likewise dismissed as mere logic of the likes of Mill. Nowadays, the attack is on the 'liberal intellectual élite'. Against this minority is supposedly the will of the people, which, according to the tabloids and many members of the House of Lords, supports Section 28 – just as Sir Frederic Thesiger warned of 'the greatest violence to the religious sentiments and feelings of the nation, if the House admitted Jews by removing the requirement of a Christian oath',[67] just as 'the Anti[suffragist]s' ultimate weapon was the referendum'[68]. But surely anti-intellectualism and populism should be no match for well-reasoned arguments? Unfortunately, they are: in another echo of history the reforming spirit of the House of Commons is confounded by the status-quo-ist House of Lords.

The similarities of yesterday's resistance to today's resistance in the move towards greater justice in law and life must make us wonder whether we are really fulfilling Margaret Thatcher's demand quoted at the outset: 'Policy-making must be firmly based on analysis of what we know to be the facts'. This is after all our democratic duty. It is demanded by our intellectual integrity. We can only regard with utmost suspicion arguments that have been deployed against three of the most fundamental movements in our democratic history. When they resurface today, we must remember the past and consign them to it as part of the battle against the rifeness of unreason at the heart of our society.

The atheist connection

But what has all this to do with atheism? The purpose of this book has been to argue for atheism by placing it within a coherent worldview which does justice both to our ignorance and to our dislike of our ignorance. Within that worldview, atheism has arisen naturally, though not inevitably, as enquiry has progressed. Furthermore, the pursuit of democracy requires the same approach that exploring and explaining the world demands:

Spartan and meritocratic. If our institutions and laws are to create and sustain equality and justice, then they must base themselves on fair consideration of the relevant facts. They may not perpetuate prejudice and ignorance immemorial. Reason, not religion, remains the ultimate arbiter.

Thus, reason, atheism, and the pursuit of democracy are all natural allies. Opposed to them are unreason and theism, forces which it has been my aim in this chapter to expose as historical hindrances, as on-going sources of error, and as the natural enemies of the pursuit of the democratic ideals to which we are committed. Whereas religious belief remains the prerogative of the individual, the state must remain committed to atheism, both in the nature of its institutions and in what forces it permits to influence its laws and legislators. To give official platform to religion is to allow into the heart of democracy anti-atheist forces and, hence, to cut the very fabric of democracy.

Chapter 7

Two Corollaries, Two Addenda, and A Note

In this final chapter, I wish to tie up some loose ends and to look directly, if briefly, at some points merely alluded to above. Two are additional arguments. Two are consequences of the arguments already presented.

The agnostic corollary

Agnosticism is the studied art of fence-sitting in face of fields neither of which offers greener grass. Alternatively, it is an absence of belief in virtue of an absence of arguments: no belief concerning God's existence because there are no compelling arguments for either atheism or theism. In arguing that 'Atheism is the plausible and probably correct belief that God does not exist' and that theism is 'the implausible and probably incorrect view that God does exist', I hope to have disproven the agnostic premise that there is an absence of compelling arguments. The agnostic may now desist from fence-sitting and start grazing in pastures green.

The accommodating atheist corollary

Accommodating atheists are slipped agnostics. They accept that God's existence is beyond proof and disproof and then deduce that the beliefs are of equal logical pedigree. Yet, for whatever reason, they profess atheism in the absence of argument. The accommodating atheist may now cease to be so accommodating, for two reasons. Firstly, atheism and theism are not of equal logical pedigree, as is seen by examining the worldviews from which they follow. Secondly, as discussed in the preceding chapter, there is a democratic duty against accommodation. And accommodating atheism minus the accommodation is, of course, just atheism.

The evil addendum

People suffer. Animals suffer. If God, the creator, is omniscient, then he knew, at the time of creation, how the world would develop. He knew he was creating a world with suffering. If God is omnipotent, he could have created things otherwise. Therefore, if God is omnipotent and omniscient, he is also nasty. Hence, there are no omnipotent, omniscient, supremely benevolent beings. The counterclaim that we suffer because of our own actions is irrelevant: what counts is that God chose to create this world, and no other, knowing that it would lead to suffering. The counterclaim that God has a plan of which our suffering is part – perhaps to disillusion us with the physical and to make us turn to the spiritual – is irrelevant: that merely makes him a deity with a plan, who chose to create this world, and no other, knowing that it would lead to suffering. The counterclaim that evil is necessary if we are to have free will is irrelevant: for the decision to create free will means that God has a plan and that merely makes him a deity with a plan, who chose to create this world, and no other, knowing that it would lead to suffering. Hence, the conclusion stands.

However, atheism does not follow. There is still space for belief in a lesser God: one that is supremely powerful but not omnipotent. This world may be the best that a supremely powerful deity can manage, for all we know. Or maybe God is only intermittently benevolent and fitfully forgetful. If that were the case, it might be best to keep on his good side. Which leads to:

The aleatoric addendum

Blaise Pascal reckoned that, if one believes in God and is wrong, then one dies and nothing is lost. But if one does not though he does, then all is lost when one dies. So, he wagered that we are better off believing in God, keeping our bases covered, as it were. This is especially so once we recognise that God might be rather imperfect: we would be well off to keep ourselves in his good books. The problem with Pascal's wager, however, is that no one knows the odds. Perhaps God prefers the honest atheist to the pandering Pascal. Perhaps God likes the drama of a conversion on the death bed after a romping life better than hermetic piety. One simply cannot tell.

A note on life: meaning and meaningfulness

Having rejected all theisms that purport to tell us the meaning of life, are we now committed to saying that life is inherently meaningless? Yes. But that is no bad thing. After all, inherently speaking, the answer just given is also meaningless. There is no inherent meaning to the word 'yes'. It is our interaction with it that imbues it with meaning. And as with 'yes', so with life. It is individuals' interaction with life, their attitudes, decisions and actions, that will ultimately make their lives meaningful. This thought may engender in some a slight fear of freedom or angst at error, a vertigo at the possibility of philosophical freefall. Yet, this is no new problem. As the theists have often informed us (especially two paragraphs higher), there is no freedom without the possibility of error. This only serves to heighten the significance of a life well lived.

Chapter 8

Conclusion

Let us hear the conclusion of the whole matter – Ecclesiastes 12:13

How does one guide an intelligent person to atheism? My assumption is that intelligent people wish to believe what is true, or, truth being hard to recognise, to believe at least what is plausible and coherent, what stands a chance of being true. My tactic, therefore, has been to embed the debate between theism and atheism in a larger and more fundamental dialogue concerning the two chief worldviews (to purloin a phrase from Galileo).

That dialogue begins by recognising that the apparently universal human urge to explain indicates two facts about ourselves: that we are ignorant and that we do not like our ignorance. A plausible worldview must reflect those facts. As such a candidate, I offered the Spartan meritocracy, a worldview of questions and justification, where the starting assumptions are Spartan, in recognition of the inevitable error inherent in any initial attempt at explanation, and where each piece of the explanation, starting assumptions included, survives on its merits and dies on its demerits, in recognition of what an explanation intuitively is. Equal and opposite to the Spartan meritocracy is the Baroque monarchy, which helps itself to an elaborate collection of starting assumptions, immune from later revision, no matter how much they are contradicted by later discoveries and realisations. Clearly, we should embrace the former and shun the latter. And from this argument, the rest of the book more or less follows.

On the one hand, we can go beyond theoretical pedigree of worldviews and look at their worth when applied. The Spartan meritocracy is as successful in practice as it is on paper. When deployed in explanation of the natural world, it has produced science, technology, mathematics, and more. When employed in practical issues, it has produced conceptions and analyses of justice, fairness, goodness, and more, that shape our society and ourselves, in both subtle and substantial ways. The Baroque monarchy, by contrast, has explained next to nothing about the natural world and has often proved quite caustic to the fabric of society and to the human weft itself.

On the other hand, we can remain with the theoretical realm and consider what relationship the worldviews bear to atheism and theism. There is no neat correlation here. Most forms of theism, including all the great religions are Baroque monarchies, yet so are some versions of atheism, such as those incorporated into the twentieth century's great totalitarianisms. On the other hand, the Spartan meritocracy can be instantiated both by Descartes' theism and the rational atheism argued for in this book. But, as rational theism has not withstood the test of time, all the Spartan meritocracies on offer now and for the foreseeable future are atheist.

Putting these two hands together, we reach this simple conclusion. Our urge to explain is met by one worldview, the Spartan meritocracy, successful in theory and practice, which commits us to atheism. Anyone who cares about truth, then, must be an atheist. To be a theist, however, to believe in God, or faith, or religion, is to embrace the implausible, to endorse the erroneous, to eschew the sensible, and shun the demonstrably successful. Theism, in short, is a pathodoxy.

Realising the pathodoxical status of religious belief ramifies beyond individuals' beliefs. It entails a moral responsibility. Appreciating the intimate relationship between pursuit of democratic ideals and Spartan, meritocratic thought, the health of our society demands that its principles and procedures, whilst safeguarding the individual's right to pathodoxy, remain at all times clearminded, clearsighted, and atheist.

I can only concur with King David: 'The fool hath said in his heart there is no God'. The intelligent person, with a wealth of reasons, would have said it out loud.

Endnotes

1. John Searle, *Mind, Language and Society* (London: 1999).
2. Denzinger-Schönmetzer, *Enchyridion symbolorum definitionum declarationum*. Cited in John Cornwell, *Hitler's Pope: The Secret History of Pius XII*, (Viking Penguin, London: 1999): page 12.
3. The problem was that previous experiments were designed to measure the speed of the earth through the ether divided by the speed of light squared. 'Squared' was the crucial part. When the experiments showed a null result, it was impossible to pin the blame on the ether. It might simply have resulted from a combination of the margin of error inherent in any experiment and the fact that near-zero numbers result from dividing anything modest by the square of anything huge, like the speed of light. Michelson and Morley avoided this problem by measuring the earth's speed divided by the speed of light unsquared.
4. Namely: the speed of light is independent of the speed of its source (you cannot give light a push); and the value of the length transformations is universal.
5. It may be more accurate to attribute the aversion to empirical methods to Aristotle's followers, who tended to regard his works as a complete theory to be dogmatically defended – a rather unscientific rationale, certainly non-meritocratic, and hardly in keeping with Aristotle's statement in the Nichomachean Ethics that fact is the ultimate arbiter.
6. Roger Swinburne offers a not so radical proposal along these lines in *The Existence of God* (Oxford 1979). It is worth mentioning here both as an example, like Descartes', if Spartan, meritocratic theism, and because it offers an alternative perspective on arguments for God's existence Swinburne claims that such arguments should not be taken as individual, perfect deductions as has been traditional. Instead, they should be taken together 'abductively', as is common in other rational enquiry. 'Arguments from observable data to an explanatory hypothesis in science, history, or any other area ... make the hypothesis probable in so far as (1) if the hypothesis is true, it is probable that the data will occur, (2) the occurrence of the data is not otherwise probable, and (3) the hypothesis is simple.' This approach shares with mine the idea of pretending at first to know little about the world and then feeding in one's accumulated knowledge gradually. In this respect and in its attempted emulation of research methods successful elsewhere, Swinburne's idea is interesting and worth

pursuing. Unfortunately, Swinburne's own pursuit, in my opinion, fails. It involves numerous arbitrary assumptions and erroneous inferences of very varied nature, which, together, deprive his specific attempt of plausibility. An alternative fleshing out of his ideas may be possible, though I doubt it. This is not, however, the place to discuss these issues. (Quotation from *The Oxford Companion to Philosophy*: page 764)

7. My favourite is Victor Hugo's statement of the puzzling mathematical nature of Einstein's universe: *Cette double mer du temps et de l'espace ... dire si son lit est de roche ou de fange.* Literally, *This double sea of time and space ... to say if its sima's of rock or of mud.* Less literally: *Space-time ... determinate or colloid?*

8. See, for instance, Philip Kitcher, *The Nature of Mathematical Knowledge* (Oxford University Press: 1984).

9. Cited in Bertrand Russell, *Why I Am Not A Christian* (Routledge: 1979): page 28.

10. Some, such as the proponents of 'Islamic Science' and 'Marxist Science', would disagree. Their opinions are discussed in Chapter 5. Radical postmodernists would also object, claiming that putative generalisations are sociolinguistic constructs masquerading as universals within a highly dominant, yet nonetheless deconstructible, scientific discourse. If you are unfortunate enough to understand what that means, then ask yourself whether the eradication of polio was a sociolinguistic construct, or whether deconstructing the term *atom bomb* would assist erstwhile inhabitants of Hiroshima. Otherwise, do not.

11. For other scientific and historical details, see Richard Feynman, *The Character of Physical Law* (MIT Press: 1967), whose exposition I partly follow below.

12. Pietro Redondi, *Galileo: Heretic* (London: 1988)

13. Cited in Pervez Hoodbhoy, *Islam and Science: Religious Orthodoxy and the Battle for Rationality* (Zed Books, London: 1991): page 25.

14. If you have never seen Mandelbrot sets, see, for instance, Heinz-Otto Peitgen and Peter Richter, *The Beauty of Fractals* (Berlin: 1986).

15. John Keats, *Ode on a Grecian Urn*.

16. In Descartes' thinking, language and God *were* related. God was clearly non-physical, and language could not be reduced to mechanics, the criterion of the physical. Hence, both God and language were related by non-physical, spiritual substance. However, Descartes did not use language to argue for God's existence. The existence of God and the relationship between God and language were different matters.

17. Bertrand Russell, *Why I Am Not A Christian* (Routledge: 1979): page 34.

18. In Brian MacArthur, *The Penguin Book of Historic Speeches* (London: 1996).

19. Anthony Storr, *Feet of Clay: A Study of Gurus* (Harper Collins, London: 1996): page xi.

20. Hitler's Table Talk.

21. Speech to the House of Lords, 15 October 1999.

22. Alan Bullock, *Hitler and Stalin: Parallel Lives* (London: 1991). He quotes from Alex de Jonge, *Stalin and the Shaping of the Soviet Union* (London 1986).

23. Rauschning, *Hitler Speaks*.

24. See, for instance, his introduction in Pervez Hoodbhoy, *Islam and Science: Religious Orthodoxy and the Battle for Rationality* (Zed Books, London: 1991).

25. Cotton farming was the exception.

26. Stephen Jay Gould, *Rocks of Ages: Science and Religion in the Fullness of Life* (New York: 1999): page 3.

27. M. H. Tester, *Hands That Heal*, (Barnie & Jenkins, London: 1970).

28. I have been unable to verify all the details in this paragraph. In case an error has slipped in, the reader may substitute *Shmayans* for *Mayans* without altering the point of the story.

29. Paramahansa Yogananda, *Man's Eternal Quest* (Los Angeles: 1982): pages 14 and 45.

30. Yogananda: page 215.

31. Another error, relevant given the discussion of Michelson, Morley, and Einstein above, is his belief in ether. It can be used to illustrate the same points.

32. Margaret Thatcher, *The Path to Power* (Harper Collins Publishers, London: 1995): page 550.

33. My chief sources have been: for slavery, Hugh Thomas' *The Slave Trade: The History of the Atlantic Slave Trade 1440-1870* (Picador, London: 1997), and James Walvin's *Black Ivory: A History of British Slavery* (Harper Collins Publishers, London: 1992); for Jewish emancipation, David Feldman's *Englishmen and Jews: Social Relations and Political Culture 1840-1914* (Yale University Press, New Haven and London: 1994); for female suffrage, Brian Harrison's *Separate Spheres: The Opposition to Women's Suffrage in Britain*, (Croom Helm, London:1978), Mrs Frederic Harrison's *The Freedom of Women: Against Female Suffrage* (Watts & Co., London 1908), and Alan P. Grimes' *The Puritan Ethic and Woman Suffrage* (New York, OUP: 1967).

34. In what follows, I shall use the term *slavery* loosely, encompassing both the slave trade and the institution of slavery itself. *Abolition* means the abolition of slavery in this loose sense.

35. Thomas: page 450.

36. Walvin: page 183. Anglicans' emphasis on theology accounts for the failure of their mission relative to continental Christian sects', which did not demand indoctrination prior to baptism.

37. Thomas: page 489.

38. Elizabeth Donnan, *Documents Illustrative of the Slave Trade to America*, (Washington, 1930): III, 7. Cited in Thomas: page 451. Emphasis added.

39. Thomas: page 457.

40. Thomas: page 449.

41. Thomas: page 452.

42. PP 1845, XIV: page 22. Cited in Feldman: page 29.
43. Raikes Currie, cited in Feldman: page 43.
44. Feldman: page 33.
45. W.J. Conybearne, 'Jewish Disabilities', *Quarterly Review*, September 1847: pages 526-7. Cited in Feldman: page 33.
46. Cited in Feldman: page 35.
47. *Hansard*, 3rd series, XCVIII, April 25, 1848. Cited in Feldman: page 38.
48. Feldman: page 41.
49. Feldman: page 47.
50. *Hansard*, 3rd series, XCV, col. 1,278, December 16, 1847.
51. B. Harrison: page 84.
52. B. Harrison: page 35.
53. Percy, *H.C. Deb.*, 30 Apr. 1873, c. 1251. Cited in B. Harrison: page 57.
54. Mrs F. Harrison: page 51. Mrs Harrison shows a warm disposition to Catholicism and its treatment of women.
55. B. Harrison: page 56.
56. Dana Greene, *Suffrage and Religious Principle: Speeches and Writings of Olympia Brown* (Scarecrow Press, London: 1983): page 2. This quotation resonates with B. Harrison's observation that British and Australian anti-suffragism comprised a strong strand of anti-intellectualism.
57. Grimes: page x.
58. Grimes: page xii.
59. Source: http://www.stonewall.org.uk/aoc/s28cp.pdf
60. Thatcher: pages 152 – 153.
61. Feldman: page 28.
62. B. Harrison: page 49.
63. Thatcher: page 150.
64. Cited in Thomas: page 490.
65. Cited in B. Harrison: page 43.
66. Mrs F. Harrison: page 50.
67. Cited in Feldman: page 35.
68. B. Harrison: page 39.

Index